LIFE LESSONS FROM DARLA

*A courageous girl living gracefully with a
terminal illness taught me to empathize
and accept people with differences*

MARY SALZ

Look Beyond
PUBLICATIONS

Life Lessons from Darla

*A courageous girl living gracefully with a terminal illness
taught me to empathize and accept people with differences*

Mary Salz

Permission requests: lookbeyondpublications.com

ISBN: 979-8-9875909-0-4 (Paperback)
ISBN: 979-8-9875909-3-5 (Large Print)
ISBN: 979-8-9875909-1-1 (Ebook)
ISBN: 979-8-9875909-2-8 (Audio)

Guidance & Assistance Sojourn Publishing, LLC
Cover Design Rebecca Wallace and Ellie Nowels
Cover Layout Ellie Nowels, Centipede Graphics
Author Photo Erin Brown Photography
Illustrations Jennifer Kalis Illustration

Author's Note

My goal in writing this book is to share with the reader what I have observed and experienced in dealing with illness, death, and other stresses and losses in my own life and to share my thoughts about coping with these challenges. I hope my observations will be helpful and encouraging. However, I also want to make it clear that I am not trained or certified as a professional counselor, and I encourage you to consult an appropriate expert if you are dealing with medical, psychological, or other issues. My book does not take the place of expert advice and assistance.

Dedications

For Darla, who was filled with light and love

For my wonderful children
May their world be more loving and kind

For all the people with differences
May they be loved for who they are, just as they are

Acknowledgments

Thank you so much to the kind people allowing
me to share a part of their lives with you

Many thanks to these wonderful people
for great amounts of love, help, and support

The Lamb Family
Doris June, Dennis, John, and Dianna,
who was steadfast and loving throughout these years

Kari, Rebecca, Ellie, Mari, Barb, Anne, Paul,
Debbie, Aria, Martha, Anya, and Denise

Much gratitude to Tom Bird and his team, for their
caring guidance in weaving my thoughts into a story

Special thanks to Rebecca Wallace and
Ellie Nowels for their beautiful cover design

Contents

Part 1
A Deep and Precious Friendship

PART 2
LIFE LESSONS FROM DARLA

A Deep and Precious Friendship

Imagine a cute young girl with sparkling blue eyes sitting on a deep shag carpet. She is looking adoringly at a ball of orange fluff in her cupped hands. As if by magic, it starts to bounce up and down! Look closely. The fluff ball has dark eyes and nose—a tiny face.

This darling dog weighs only two pounds and can fit into a pocket, or a teacup. Petie is an apricot-colored teacup poodle and will be no larger than five pounds. Grinning playfully, the girl kisses the wiggly little pup and sets him on the ground to wildly circle around her. He's so small he is nearly lost in the long carpet and his movements are

wobbly. She is having the time of her life, laughing so hard she falls down beside him. He bounces at her many times only to roll away, until he joyfully lands on top of her and returns her kisses with great enthusiasm. Petie can entertain for hours and sweetly snuggle with this happy child, who is his favorite person in the entire world.

Another dog in the family, Angel, is a much larger Standard poodle. The difference between the two poodles is comical. Little Petie is not even the size of Angel's head! Angel likes Petie but sometimes she needs a break from the energetic antics of the puppy. The two dogs will be dyed pink and adorned with colorful ribbons at Easter time. Sometimes the ribbons go around their ears, looking like pigtails, and sometimes the ribbons circle a topknot. The young girl considers the dogs her very close friends and truly appreciates them. She likes that poodles are smart. They are easily trained and make good therapy dogs. In fact, more than being cute and funny, Petie is an emotional support dog. He provides priceless service to his owner, who has cancer. His main roles are to love her and make her feel better. She loves her poodles, her friends. In fact, she treats all animals as her friends and they all like her!

DARLA

I'd like to introduce you to this sweet girl who loved animals—my friend, Darla. This is a story about Darla and me, a friendship that flourished for six incredible years. During that time, we enjoyed ourselves immensely. We also discovered that life is about being transformed during challenges. I learned many things in my younger years with my dear friend and cherish our time spent together.

Darla was born in Tempe, Arizona in the 1950s, in the "Valley of the Sun". She was a cute little girl with soft blue eyes and light brown hair. Her parents, brother, and sisters idolized her, the baby of the family. She and her sister, Dianna, were close in age and often played together. When Darla was very young, her family moved into a new home community. Many families with children soon joined the neighborhood.

There was a wonderful Olympic-size city swimming pool just a few miles from her desert home. It was always full of happy people. The water sparkled when touched by the bright sun. The pool area was aptly named Tempe Beach, though there was no sand to be found. It was concrete with sections of green grass and reclining pool

3

chairs, for those watching kids or getting a tan. It was a very inviting place when the temperatures soared into the hundreds. Darla's family would often take refuge in this concrete oasis. A dip in the refreshing water made them forget the blazing Arizona sun for a while. She loved to swim and couldn't imagine anything better than to spend all day jumping off the springy diving board and merrily splashing around in the cool water.

Darla was lucky to have a caramel-colored Shetland pony, Pepe. She helped care for Pepe at her grandparents' home, feeding him hay and brushing his thick coat and shaggy mane. He could be ornery and sometimes would even bite, but with his special person, he was even-tempered and nice. They just understood each other. Darla had an extraordinary way with all animals, a whisperer, as they say. She seemed to talk to animals without actually speaking. Her nature was gentle and loving, so Pepe became sweet and calm around her. Because of his short legs and wide back, it was easy for her to climb on to ride. He let her lie down on him so she could hug his neck and lovingly pet his long brown mane. When she rode, she and her pony moved as one, delighting in each other's company.

With her loving family and their many animals, Darla was very content, calm, and carefree. She was often quiet, but not in a meek way. She was self-assured and contemplative. As a nature lover, she enjoyed being outside. Sharing that love, her family often went on outdoor adventures such as camping, boating on the nearby lakes, and floating down the river in inner tubes. Due to her sunny and easy disposition, she was happy doing almost anything.

Though she was often quiet and calm, there were times when Darla got bored. She would then dream up interesting things to do. When her imagination was in motion, she became too quiet. She was plotting. Her fun and feisty side was ready to burst out. Her usual soft smile changed into a smirk. Those blue eyes started to twinkle delightedly and it became clear that she was planning something a bit mischievous or something amusing—to her. Upon seeing these changes, you might think, *Oh no, now what will happen?*

MARY

I moved to the dry, dusty Phoenix area from the green and rainy Midwest in the 1960s. What a change! My father had been in the Army Air Corps, stationed in Arizona. He loved the state. He enjoyed traveling all around Arizona to see the different landscapes—cacti, mountains, red rocks, and tall pine trees. He couldn't wait to get back and eventually decided to move his family there. The rest of us were not quite sure about moving from the Midwest. But Dad insisted, "The desert just grows on you. You'll love it!" He told us about all its great features. He even made the rattlesnakes sound exciting. The older kids would roll their eyes but the younger two, myself included, started buying into it. A real adventure! I couldn't wait to see this wondrous place! After all, I was only in the second grade. I didn't have the bonds the older children had with friends and cousins and, in addition, I really didn't understand the permanence of the move. To me, it seemed more like a thrilling long vacation. Though sad to leave my relatives and my two special friends, I was willing to try this great place that Dad so loved. As a bonus, we would get a chance to better know our Southwestern relatives on our dad's side of the family.

Bright and early one summer morning (actually still dark), Dad called out, "The bus is leaving!" Seven of us sleepily climbed into our station wagon. It was equipped with two bench seats and a wayback, a third area that was like an open trunk or hatchback. The wayback was fought over since it was farther away from our parents and stocked with blankets and pillows. We could relax and look out the back. With little room inside, some of our luggage was piled up and strapped to the top of the car, much like in the movie *National Lampoon's Vacation.* We crossed our fingers that it would stay there throughout the whole journey. That was not to be. On a long stretch of road, someone yelled from the back, "Hey, Dad, the luggage is falling off!" Back we went to collect it, piece by piece. We were lucky one of the kids riding in the wayback was awake! Amid the many squabbles typical of five kids stuck in very close quarters for sixteen hours a day, we did it. In two long, crazy days, we had moved halfway across the country.

Life is ever-changing, like a kaleidoscope. You roll along and experience some bright, wonderful things and also have some darker times. During the darker times, look toward the light and things look better and brighter. Moving was my first big change in life. Where would it lead?

There I was, in Arizona! My eyes went wide when I saw the majestic mountains surrounding the Valley of the Sun, especially at sunset. The colors were amazing—pink, orange, dark blue, and purple. The large mountains appeared dark when silhouetted against the intense colors. Quite a picture, just like the postcards of beautiful sunsets. My favorite sight was Camelback Mountain, which looked like a camel lying down. I couldn't help but wonder how this was created. Nature had always interested me and this was fascinating. The Midwest was mostly flat land or rolling hills. It was hard to imagine how these huge Phoenix mountains just came up so high from the surrounding flat land. I pondered this for a long while before I learned about volcanic and tectonic processes. Even after learning geology, it seemed like a miracle. We went to the Desert Botanical Garden to see and learn about many desert plants. Cacti are so interesting. They are made for the desert. They have prickly spines for protection from animals and the sun. The spines also help with water conservation. We learned to be careful of those little spikes. Some are barbed and can really hurt. The jumping cactus, cholla, doesn't truly jump. However, the spines come off easily and can get into people who get too close. My aunt had an unfortunate encounter with one during a visit. It was very painful! Pulling spines out of straying basketballs wasn't fun either. All cacti can flower. Many bloom annually or more often, but some don't until they are decades old and then only under perfect conditions. Some attract tiny, beautiful hummingbirds. We once had a tiny hummingbird nest on some wind chimes on our porch. It was very cute, but we got dive-bombed by the mama, as a warning to stay away. This was all new to me. I much enjoyed seeing all the changes and differences in the wonderful cacti.

I missed the bright green, lush trees of my old home but the grayish green trees were nice and, like my father, I was intrigued by the different cacti and wildflowers in Phoenix as well as the varied landscapes of the state. I loved the tall Ponderosa pine forests that made me feel so small, as well as the huge and magnificent red rock formations that were named for their shapes, like Bell, Cathedral, Snoopy, and Ship Rocks. Being young, Snoopy Rock (from the *Peanuts* cartoon) was my favorite. There he was with his nose and feet pointing skyward, as if lying on his doghouse. He looked as if he were chiseled from the rock. How could nature create such a perfect sculpture? Incredible. We could drive just a few hours from the Phoenix area and see totally different landscapes, even ski areas. I understood why Dad loved the state!

A new environment and new kids were scary but also exciting! Before moving, we were often told of the many children living in our new neighborhood. I couldn't wait to find them. So, when on a clear summer day I stood looking up and down the street and saw *nobody*, I was perplexed. Where were they? Not one kid to be seen. I was so disappointed! I soon found out the reason kids were missing from the streets. It was June—in the desert. In June, the temperature in Phoenix is in the hundreds and can even get to 120 degrees at times. This is not an ideal time for anyone to be riding bikes and running around outside. Unlike Midwestern kids in the summer, these kids were mostly indoors or in swimming pools. Many people had swimming pools at their homes. Fun! But how would I meet all of these wonderful kids? And when I did, would I fit in and be accepted?

Best Friends

I lucked out. I quickly met an ideal playmate right down the street. I met Darla! We were inseparable. We had an immediate connection. I met someone I felt I knew deep down, a soulmate. What a joy it was to find such a friend! My fears of moving to a new place had melted away. I skipped past the multiple cacti and palo verde trees, past the mere six houses to her house, laughing as my new rubber flip-flops slapped with every step. I was just grinning from ear to ear and singing to myself, "I've got a best friend! I've got a best friend!" She gave me the gift of acceptance and true friendship. I didn't even have to try to fit in with her. I never had to be anyone but myself. The ability to be yourself and be accepted is a gift beyond words. I had never been so happy, so content. We quickly settled into a very comfortable camaraderie and enjoyed a completely blissful summer, playing and getting to know each other well.

There were so many cool things to do. We were carefree and life was good! We watched Darla's dad caring for their animals in his mini-farm in their large backyard and giggled at my dad watering our lawn in his bright yellow shorts. We helped our mothers make our favorite cookies—hot and gooey chocolate chip! First, we'd take a deep breath to take in the enticing aroma and then sink our teeth into the warm, soft cookies. Mmm … heaven! They were quick to put them away since they knew we would otherwise be eating all of them. We created art in the Girls' Club, rode bikes on the wide neighborhood streets, and played hide-and-seek outside in the dark corners of our porches before we were aware of the black widow spiders that hung out there. We tried hopping on pogo sticks, skateboarding, and rollerskating, but neither of us was great at those. We stuck to jump ropes, bikes, and hopscotch. We played with Troll dolls, Barbie dolls, and Darla's realistic but small model horses. Sometimes her Barbies pranced her horses around the family room. Often, with her sister Dianna, we made forts out of tables and sheets, played card and board games, sang to records, and watched TV shows like *Mr. Ed*, about a smart and feisty "talking" horse. Mr. Ed truly was smart. How many horses have you seen that could dial a rotary telephone using a pencil stuck between their teeth? He did it like a quadriplegic might use a mouth stick to type on a computer. His trainer was smart, too, since he was able to teach Ed to move his lips as if talking and many other tricks. Darla loved that show!

We went to the refreshing Tempe Beach pool as often as we could. We had great times playing Marco Polo, diving for big plastic rings, and doing cannonballs off the diving board, hoping for the biggest splashes. When my brother played baseball at Tempe Beach Park, we would go and play on the very old cobblestone and concrete bleachers. The terraced seats were long, wide, and safe so our parents could just let us climb around, often playing follow-the-leader. The multicolored round cobblestones sunken into the front of the concrete were very pretty to me, in a natural sense. The weathered stones had been worn down to be very smooth, unlike the old, uneven concrete. When climbing got boring, we'd listen for the brownish-gray desert toads to call, letting us know where they were. It was fun to catch them. Occasionally, Darla would decide to get some amusement by presenting a toad to some unsuspecting kids. She would impishly grin, conceal one in her cupped hands, and jog over to show off her new friend. "Want to see what I found?" Her grin turned wider when she heard the expected squeals. Some kids would pet it and some would scamper away in fear or disgust. Disgust? We thought they were kind of cute. She would release the toad close to where it had been taken, softly saying, "Hop home!"

Above all, we enjoyed eating ground-up ice in tapered paper cups. We loved to mix syrup flavors. We had to eat fast. The ice would quickly melt and the sticky stuff would dribble out the pointy bottom all over us. Parents weren't happy about sticky bodies, clothes, and cars. Unfortunately, they didn't have girls' ball games in the 1960s, but I was glad we didn't have to run in that heat. People say Phoenix feels like being in an oven in June and that's exactly how it feels. Dry and hot! Then the monsoon storms could come a month or two later and it would be more like a sauna. We'd be sweaty and thirsty just walking to each other's homes in the summer.

For living with the high heat for a few months, we got to enjoy nice weather for the rest of the year, especially in the winter. Our Midwestern relatives, acclimated to cold temperatures, would sunbathe in January when we would be in sweaters and jackets. Winter was great for running around, biking, and hiking. The flip side of stifling June, kids played outside in the winter months, when it was cool and comfortable. We could drive up into the mountains if we wanted to be cold and see snow.

We had plenty to do inside and out. Sometimes, when we were tired or simply in a quiet mood, we would decide to sit and chat in Darla's family room on the curved lounge chair. It was perfectly sized for two little girls. We'd lean back, put our feet up, and relax into talk mode. It is wonderful to have someone with whom to share secrets and view life. Eight-year-olds have much to ponder.

Much as we disliked it, our blissful summer ran into— school time. I was extremely nervous to be going to a new school. I had adjusted to living in a new place and here came more changes. I had new worries about fitting in. Even riding the big yellow bus to school was scary. I had never ridden a bus to school. Everyone stops talking and stares at the new kids as they get on. I kept my head down and made myself smile as I slipped into a seat. I didn't look up, unable to look into all the curious eyes I felt watching me. I was so glad Darla would be getting on at the next stop. When she stepped onto that bus, I lit up and scooted over for her to sit by me.

She was sweet and introduced me to a few people but, being extremely shy, for many days I stayed right by her whenever I could. I felt like a lost little pup and acted like one, following her constantly. The poor girl couldn't shake me off. I was beyond thrilled that we were in the same classroom. Just like her pony, her presence calmed me. Often we would just look across at each other and grin, knowing what the other was thinking or just happy to have a good friend nearby. During that year, I was in a special group of children who learned a Spanish story with songs. The extra content was designed to keep us from getting bored. Darla had a harder time in school. At first, it was difficult for me to understand why Darla couldn't be with me in the group. Did I want to be in a group she couldn't be in? I didn't want her to feel left out. I was encouraged to accept it and did, with her blessing. She understood and didn't appear to mind my bonus class. I think she even enjoyed listening to me practice, though she might have been smiling at how I pronounced the Spanish words. Maybe my singing amused her? Spanish was new to me so it was lots of fun while educational. We didn't make it a big thing, but learning ability was a difference between us. Though Darla took the lead in most things, I was able to help her with schoolwork.

As promised, there were many nice kids in our neighborhood. Eventually, I got to know them and had several good friends, but Darla was my best friend. I practically lived at her house. Like my house, hers was busy, with many people coming and going. We had two very social families. I believe Darla and I were the quietest in each home. Darla's family gave me a warm welcome, accepting my shyness and nervous giggling. I became comfortable with everything except the animals in their backyard. Darla's father, John, raised many animals, including pea-fowl, rabbits, and chickens. Not being used to animals, I was afraid and steered clear of them. The peacocks were beautiful but they could be aggressive. Like me, Dianna avoided them. Darla, the animal lover, was happy to be with them and feed them. I would watch out the back windows and see those nutty birds running around crazily and shake my head in awe as she calmly walked around tossing food. Every now and then it appeared a bird would be getting sassy. She would just stop and give them a look that said, "Cool it." After a second, no more sass. Animals can sense fear or anger. She had neither. They must have felt Darla's serenity because they never acted up. Even the little gray lizards that sunbathed on the concrete block walls didn't seem to move away from her. Those tiny two-inch lizards in Arizona are adorable, but they are skittish and usually dart away quickly when someone gets too close. Darla, the animal whisperer, was able to get close to any animal.

When young, I was limited to calm and small pets, like goldfish and very small turtles. They may not have been the most exciting of creatures, but I loved them. The turtles were more fun than the fish. I had a bowl that resembled a beach. The turtles needed to be out of the water at times for their health so, in the middle of the bowl, there was a platform they could crawl up and onto. The area had a tiny palm tree so they appeared to be sunbathing under the palm—pretty cute. They were only about two inches long, colored in greens and creamy browns. We raced them on the bathroom counter, in lanes made with bobby pins. As we expected, they had a hard time understanding the rules of the game. We had to keep steering them back into their lanes as they constantly veered off the course. It's tough to train tiny turtles.

It was fun to do things at Darla's house that I couldn't often do at my stricter home—like eat fast food and stay up late playing games and watching TV. There was a Jack-in-the-Box hamburger and taco restaurant just a few blocks away. I had never seen a taco. The folded snacks were different and good! Dianna, Darla, and I could walk up alone which made us feel very grown up. We would sit outside and frequently see people we knew. It was a great neighborhood hangout. I can still smell their secret sauce. Mmm. That's a scent-based memory that always makes me smile, like the buttery popcorn Dad made for my family on Friday nights when we watched *The Flintstones* on TV. We liked to eat. There was a Woolworth in our nearby shopping center with an old-fashioned soda fountain and red swivel stools. We would twirl around while eating—chocolate ice cream! As we got older, we were allowed to walk up to the new indoor mall, Los Arcos. It was a bit over a mile away. The mall had some beautiful Spanish art and architecture. There is nothing that makes a young person feel more mature than the freedom of going places without an adult. I remember sauntering up there, feeling very cool.

At Darla's, I heard about things like hockey games and saw a silver-colored Christmas tree with colorful and shiny ornaments. Rotating colored lights were shining on it, making it come to life. To me, that was quite exotic, like the peacocks. But I loved our real Christmas trees. Dad often got a forest permit and took us up to the mountains to cut down our own tree. Oh, another delightful aroma—fresh, fragrant evergreen trees. Sometimes the trees were covered with beautiful, powdery snow—something we very rarely saw in Phoenix. It was a great pleasure to walk in the woods and choose the perfect pine or fir to come home with us! We would carefully wrap it with rope to keep it safe and make it easier to manage. Then we'd drag it to the station wagon, tie it to the roof, and head back to the desert. With all the pageantry it deserved, the tree was placed for all to see, in front of the big picture window in the living room. Mom had lovely special ornaments—angels, instruments, manger scenes, and brightly decorated globes. After the lights and ornaments were added, we gently hung the single strands of silver tinsel instead of what we wanted to do—just toss it in clumps. Hanging tinsel individually is truly a lesson in patience. When everything was finished, we lit up the tree and enjoyed it. Since I saw Darla's silver tree so often, it was as if I got to have two trees that were nothing alike. Fun!

We enjoyed going to the movies. There was a nearby theater for quiet indoor viewing. That was good, but outdoor drive-in movies were great entertainment! The drive-in theaters made it easier for some people to see a movie. Parents didn't need a babysitter. Small kids could fall asleep in their pajamas and active kids didn't have to be still. People with disabilities could be in the comfort of their cars with any needed equipment. Many people even took pets. Quite a sight—the huge screen in front of all the lined-up cars and speakers on poles, ready to be put onto the car windows to provide the sound. When it was cold outside, we'd sit inside the car snuggled up in blankets. We'd warm up with wonderful hot chocolate with marshmallows floating on top. In the summer, we would sit outside under the starry, cloudless sky. Too hot in the car, we sat on the hood of the car or in lawn chairs in front of the car happily munching on buttered popcorn and drinking ice-cold sodas. We watched the people as well as the movies. Sometimes the people were more interesting—all different shapes, sizes, walks, voices, clothes, etc. The differences were fascinating. It was loud at the outdoor movies with babies crying, people talking, and dogs barking. The crunch of gravel mixed with the sound of flip-flops as people walked to get concessions. The irresistible aromas of popcorn and hot dogs lured many over to the treats. What a symphony of sensations. It could be annoying to some, but we loved it. We were most happy on the hood of the car, leaning back against the front window, our heads propped up by pillows or blankets. We felt like royalty. It was perfect.

Perfect until summer again turned to … school time. Like many kids, we were excited about activities and dreaded the schoolwork. Off we went. In class pictures, we sat side by side in the front row, where we shorter people were placed. Darla was in blue. I was in pink. We both had blue eyes and a smattering of light freckles. What was her most charming feature? That nice little smile, sometimes just a hint of a smile. So very sweet. Who would guess that a mischievous girl was inside? There were times those soft blue eyes would turn bright and gleeful, betraying her thoughts. She had some enjoyment in mind. To me, she was deliciously mischievous. Her spunk was an often hidden but fun trait, and something that would help her greatly in her future.

Differences

At some point in grade school, some kids started teasing and name calling— "tin grin" for someone with braces, "red" for red hair, "four eyes" for someone with eyeglasses, "skinny, fatty, freckles, shorty, stretch, …" It was never-ending. Who was perfect? What was normal? We were all made up of many different and special traits. So why was there all of this teasing? I didn't understand it. Was it fun for them to tease? Were they insecure? Were they trying to be funny, at the expense of others? Why be mean? When they were younger kids, they didn't care at all how someone looked. Acceptance of everyone was natural. Wouldn't it be wonderful if that young innocence and natural acceptance had remained with everyone? I truly missed the days before we had to worry about how we looked.

We should be with people as we are with nature, enjoying differences. Nothing in nature is perfect, and yet—it's perfect! Look at saguaro cacti. It would be boring if they were all the same. Instead, some have no arms, some have multiple arms, some arms grow upward, some grow downward, and some arms are quite twisted. Some saguaros have many "heads" on top. Interesting!

The same with the red rocks—what if they all looked like bells? Boring. Variations are intriguing.

People naturally have different preferences. Some like trees and some like cacti. Some like rain and others enjoy sunshine. Some people are attracted to thin people; others prefer heavier ones. My father called my friend a name—chicken legs. I was upset. Her legs were thin. So what? I told him that a couple of people told me they thought she was beautiful. To support this, I brought up currently famous models, like Twiggy. Obviously, many found their thinness very attractive though my father may have thought they were too thin. The phrase "to each his own" is quite true. It's a good thing we have varied preferences in physical traits. Interestingly, we seem to want everyone the same and different at the same time. We may be more comfortable with people who look like ourselves and think similarly, and yet, differences are exciting. That is one reason we travel. Ah, humans.

Darla and I got our biggest teasing from being small, which didn't bother us very much. Darla had a slight lisp and I had clunky support shoes. We didn't care. If we were teased, we had each other and knew we were unconditionally accepted. I only remember a couple of kids with differences that really stood out and we tried to be especially nice to them. That was Darla's specialty, taking in the underdog—like me as a shy new kid. It is amazing how little attention we pay to imperfections when we care for someone. We either don't pay attention to a difference or we appreciate the difference, as it's what makes someone special.

Acceptance has always been an issue for some people. In the 1960s, if someone had a disability or disfigurement, they were sometimes separated from everybody else. There were separate schools for them. These schools were likely established to give people with disabilities more fitting equipment and specially trained teachers and they may still be necessary for some. However, some people with differences may have been kept apart so that other people would not be uncomfortable. Perhaps the separation was to shelter them, so they wouldn't be hurt by others. Some people walled themselves off to shield themselves from the pain of teasing and bullying. They may have felt they were controlling their situations.

Some people didn't separate from others. These rare people went out doing what they needed and wanted to do despite having differences, large or small. A good change is more and more people being open now. Many people are less fearful about being seen as different.

We've come a long way. Often people venture out looking different from the norm. In fact, many people have gone the opposite, looking different on purpose to show their individuality. For them, looking unusual is an art. It is common now to see people with pink, green, or blue hair; or with clothing vastly different from what might be expected. People can have jewelry anywhere—tongues, belly buttons, noses, wherever. I remember my mom thought it was terrible when I got my ears pierced. She was not happy when my daughter was allowed to pierce her ears. Piercing is a choice that doesn't hurt anyone else. Why not? People can have their entire bodies covered in tattoos. I don't want tattoos myself, but I think some are cool. Unfortunately, not everyone understands or accepts these practices. Some still have problems with anyone different from themselves, in thoughts or looks. We need to come much further in acceptance, but it seems we are moving toward tolerance and greater acceptance in many ways. I had an interesting conversation the other day with a friend who works with teens. Teenagers seem to show acceptance of many types of diversity today but still seem uncomfortable with disabilities. Perhaps this is because disability or physical differences of this sort are often tied to illness and, at their age, illness isn't comfortable. Many teens still don't talk about it and don't want to.

In 2021, the World Health Organization stated on its website, "Over one billion people live with some form of disability." It is reported that the population is around eight billion. So—one in eight people have a disability. Wow. If we don't fit into that group ourselves, chances are good that we know someone with a difference. Increased acceptance of any sort is a step in the right direction. We can hope acceptance of disabilities keeps improving.

An Adventurous Friend

I was so happy when I was with Darla. We had fun doing the usual things and playing with the dogs, especially when their hair was dyed pink as people do now. Most of the time, we completely agreed on what to do. However, I was uncomfortable some of the times she felt more adventurous. One time, she looked around to be sure everybody was busy and then got out the telephone book. She took it into her parents' room, beckoning me to follow. "Let's do something new. I've been wanting to do this for a while." Her eyes were sparkling. A wide smile … *Oh, oh,* I thought with a cringe, *There's that look!* She had decided that fourth grade would be a great time to call the boys she liked. "Boys?" I stammered. "That's a terrible idea. Don't tell them I'm here. I'll be embarrassed!" Of course, I knew immediately—that was a big mistake. She snickered and got that gleam in her eye so I knew she took it as a challenge. She swiveled to look straight at me, smirked, and thumbed through the book to find a number. I just stared at her. My eyes got wider with each number dialed on that rotary phone—whir, click, whir, click, whir, click …. Part of me was in awe, part of me was curious, and part of me just wanted to run. The curious part took over. Would she really do this?? She would. She thought it was hilarious to start with, "Mary and I wanted to talk to you." She pushed the phone toward me and I mumbled, "Um, hi", showing my strong conversational skills. Clearly, I hadn't inherited my father's gift of gab. Darla grimaced as if mortified by my lack of poise. She quickly pulled back the phone and draped herself across the bed, gleefully chatting away, her eyes gleaming. I simply sat back in awe, amazed by her poise, and vowed never again to go near her when she had a telephone book in hand.

She grew to adore the phone. There was a common joke at the time. Prince Albert was a brand of tobacco sold in a can. She loved to call the stores to ask if they had Prince Albert in a can. When they said "Yes," she would quickly say, "Then let him out!" I'm sure the stores' employees were not happy at all, hearing this multiple times daily from various kids. Darla had a great time and laughed like crazy.

One day, Darla's mother, Ruth, found makeup all over the bathroom. Because Darla loved makeup and dressing up, there was no question as to who did it. She blamed her dog. Many parents know the classic excuse—the dog did it! The dog, however, wasn't wearing smeared lipstick and wasn't the one looking guilty.

Darla really showed her daring spirit when Dianna won a prize from a local children's television show. She won a shiny red Thunderbird Junior car! The miniature convertible held two small people and ran on a battery. It was the talk of the town, at least for the kids. They lived in a perfect place for it, a cul-de-sac with five homes. The center circle was perfect for them to be on a street yet away from real traffic. On their inaugural drive, Dianna and Darla were beeping the horn, beaming and waving at the neighbors and friends who had gathered to watch. As would be expected, everyone begged for a ride. It was really fun! This perfect cul-de-sac, however, was not exciting enough for Darla. One day, she persuaded a reluctant Dianna to go down the street and into the huge parking lot of our shopping center. Dianna was too nice to say no to the little scamp. Leaving their cul-de-sac in that tiny red car, they tootled down our street and crossed an even busier street to get to the parking lot. It was exciting and scary for Dianna. A tiny vehicle with two small occupants amid full-sized cars darting every which way is not a safe adventure. Darla didn't think much about that. For Darla? Not so scary. FUN! To top it off, the car ran out of charge and stopped in the lot. The girls didn't know enough about cars to anticipate running out of "gas." Naturally, their parents were pretty upset. I was very glad not to be involved in that adventure!

We had good times in that parking lot when carnivals were set up there. Much of the huge parking lot was unused so each year a carnival would come. Rides and booths, lights and sounds and smells—oh my! It was great! For added excitement, we would ask them to start us spinning before they started us moving around on one of the rides. We would stuff ourselves with terribly unhealthy, wonderful food! Since it was right at the end of our street, we knew many of the people there and got to go more than once each year. We had a nice life with few worries or responsibilities.

In the fifth grade, Darla and I were assigned to a male teacher. A male teacher! I have no idea why but I was terrified. I begged my mother to get me out of this scary situation. She rolled her eyes and wisely said, "No. You will have to deal with challenges throughout your life. You will cope and you will be fine." I was petrified. Darla wasn't at all fazed. Bring him on! On the very first day, she was reprimanded. Of course, we were sitting side by side. She put her desk lid up so Mr. Spencer couldn't see her and proceeded to whisper to me. Grimacing, I thought, *Oh thanks, add to my stress.* He soon focused on her open desk and my reddening face. He kept talking as he slowly walked toward us. My eyes darted back and forth between them. I couldn't pay attention to what either of them was saying. Darla was totally oblivious to the fact that I was extremely nervous, slightly shaking my head "no." The other kids were quietly chuckling. He carefully put her desk lid down with a soft clunk and told her that we needed to pay attention when he was speaking. She just nodded her head, her lips slowly moving into a smirk. She was fearless, my friend. She was never really bad or hurtful, just mischievous at times.

Just as Mr. Spencer was calm the first day, he was always wonderful with us. I could have let my fear change something really great in my life. I'm very glad I wasn't allowed to change classes. He was just starting his career and was one of my best teachers. He really liked his students. Despite their tangle on the first day, he and Darla had a special bond. They were similar in nature, peace lovers. I think he secretly enjoyed her feisty side, too.

Changes

During that year, Darla and I grew apart. A new girl moved in across the street and she and Darla didn't seem to get along. Despite my attempts to get Darla to go over to her home with me, she wasn't interested. I was torn between friends. I liked the new girl. I understood how she felt in a new place and wanted to help her. We became very good friends. Though I was happy to make a new friend, I felt bad that I couldn't be as good a friend to Darla. Sometimes it happens like that with friends. New people can come in and change the dynamic of a relationship. Friends may grow apart, but the friendship doesn't have to end. Sometimes friends grow distant and, even decades later, they become connected again, as if no time has passed at all! Luckily, Darla and I stayed friends and we only had to wait a short time for an opportunity to become close again.

In sixth grade, our elementary school brains were often excitedly thinking about moving up to the big time— middle school! Everyone was talking about all that we would do there. Yes, we would be the little guys on campus, but what opportunities awaited us! Dances, sports, new kids, boyfriends … boyfriends? Maybe Darla would date one of the boys she had called years earlier. We were so excited. We couldn't wait for the following year.

Unfortunately, toward the middle of the year, our excitement was disrupted. Darla had a bump on her knee and we got the news that it could be cancerous. What? How could that be? She was in the sixth grade. People got cancer when they were old, or so we thought, if we thought about it at all. Now we were forced to think about it. Kids sometimes got sick. Sometimes they got cancer.

At first, Darla had some tests. She was nervous because they had to take out a bit of the lump to test it, a biopsy. Waiting was hard. We wanted to ignore it, and we went on with our lives, but a question was hanging out there. Was she okay? Darla waited and waited, then finally had an answer. Cancer. Scary. In fact, they didn't use that word in front of Darla. Anything sounded better than cancer. What next? More tests. More waiting. Then, she had chemotherapy and radiation to treat her disease. Her life abruptly changed the instant she got the diagnosis. As a twelve-year-old, she was not ready for anything like this. Shock. Disbelief. Heart pounding with emotions changing so quickly that it was hard to keep up. After some emotions played through, reality set in. But it was really a questionable reality. Sometimes it seemed like being in a cloud. Things were real but fuzzy. There were too many emotions at the same time. Taking it in took time and patience. I saw and heard so much of what she went through to cope and yet I'm sure I just got the tip of her emotions. How could someone else totally understand?

A cold shiver went through me as I was told the diagnosis. I let out a huge breath that I didn't realize I was holding while I processed the information. I also went through an emotional roller coaster. When I finally calmed down, I understood what really mattered. Our friendship was unconditional. I would be there in good times and in bad. I would rather hold my vomiting friend than do my favorite thing with someone I didn't care for. My friend was really sick and needed me. I knew she needed me but I didn't have any idea what help looked like. I would definitely be there but what could I do? My mother often helped people. I asked her what I could do. She said that it's best to ask what in particular is needed. Do they need meals, medicines picked up, or rides for the other children? I understood and agreed, but I asked again, "What I should do as a kid, a friend?" "Just be there for her," was her logical answer. Simple. Wait … simple? It should be but isn't.

People get caught up in not knowing what to say, what to do. What if we do something wrong? What if we can't hide bad feelings? We don't want to be there because it will be uncomfortable. I thought, *Will I say the wrong thing or look silly just sitting there? Maybe I'll see something I don't want to see. I don't like needles. I don't like to see blood.* Whatever goes on in our heads can stop us from being there. However, the sick person doesn't get a choice. None of us likes anything to do with illness.

We need to be there anyway. We don't need any answers or great words. I knew nothing to say. I knew I wasn't going to solve anything, but I could go visit her and do things with her. I could help take her mind away from it all for a while. I could help her feel like a regular kid. Of course, I felt anxious, but it made me feel less upset to try, to just be there. Nobody saw this illness coming. Our lives were suddenly seriously altered and it was mind-boggling.

Darla and her family were thrown into an existence where helping Darla to get better was their priority. Doctors, nurses, and other medical people were now people they got to know well. School was important but nothing held the same urgency as curing her cancer. Less important things were pushed aside. Her mother spent most of her energy and focus on helping her little girl. The rest of the family did what they could to help while still working and going to school. I went about my life by going to school and seeing friends, but Darla was always on my mind. I truly felt like a person split in two, wanting to be with her and also to do other things. I prayed for her and went to see her whenever I could.

The Role of a Friend

It could seem to others like Darla's life had stopped, but it hadn't. It did change from the way she knew it, but she was the same person inside. It was hard for her to be so separated. Isolated. Long days and nights at the hospital or at home, missing school and friends. Socially cut off. Sometimes she showed how downhearted she was. She was depressed and lonely. She was still a kid and needed to play. Dianna and her other siblings were with her, but they had school and other commitments. Her mother stayed with her almost non-stop, but she wasn't a kid. Her father worked. I couldn't imagine how boring it would be to stay home all the time. I had only a week or two in second grade when I was unable to move from a bed or couch, due to an infection. That was hard enough. I hated it. I felt sorry for myself because I couldn't go out trick or treating. She endured many months of this isolation from friends and fun.

Darla had a difficult time with all the medical procedures. They hurt her or made her feel sick. Many people don't understand what a person is going through during cancer treatments. Exhaustion and pain can be invisible yet extremely difficult to endure. I didn't need to understand everything she was going through, I just needed to know that things were really hard for her. They explained only that she got medicine that would very likely make her sick and often tired. Indeed it did. I couldn't physically help her, though I dearly wished I could take away her pain! My important roles were to love her and keep her connected to the wider world, especially when she couldn't go to school and some other friends couldn't be with her. I was happy to do that. We did many of the things we had enjoyed earlier, before her illness. She loved chocolate and we often played games while eating chocolate. That I could do for her. I could absolutely eat chocolate for her.

I could also listen. At times, I looked deeply into her eyes and could see rawness, eyes clouded with emotion. She needed to talk yet was reluctant. She knew she was safe to be herself with me, but it was still hard for her to open up. Sometimes I felt that maybe she didn't want to admit to herself that she had bad feelings. Maybe she feared I wouldn't be able to take it and would stop coming. I just didn't feel right accepting an "I'm fine. We don't need to talk about it." It seemed too easy for her to dismiss or bury feelings. So, when it seemed the right time and place, I would gently but forcibly say, "Tell me." There really was no sense in her keeping things hidden if she could let it out with someone who cared. And I wasn't going anywhere, no matter what she told me! If she seemed unsure, I would say something like, "You couldn't shake me off when I was so afraid in third grade and you can't shake me off now. I can take whatever you throw at me. Spit it out." Then I'd lift my chin high and try to look tough, which just made her smirk and roll her eyes at me. Perfect. Laughing at me opened her up. It was even okay if she wanted to complain. Good heavens, anyone would need to complain while going through chemo. Sometimes she would let out fears or frustration. *"Yes!"* I'd think, "*Maybe I can ease some of her troubles, at least for a short time."* I was no counselor but I was a good listener. I tried to comfort and encourage her, with words or with hugs. Sometimes she encouraged me. She realized it wasn't all about her. Those who loved her were also in pain, emotionally. She was quite concerned with others and how they felt. It seemed as though her illness and confinement made her even more aware of others' troubles. Sometimes, it was right to just be together and be silent. It could be relaxing to be quiet together. Undemanding. Silence is uncomfortable for many people, especially in our noisy, fast-paced society. Even so, sometimes silence is needed. Silence is welcome. Other times, it was right to let Darla do all the talking. It seems that people can get caught up in trying to fix things. Often, ill or upset people just need to get their feelings or thoughts out. No answers are needed or even wanted. The best listeners can do just that. Listen. Without talking. I mostly let her control the communication. She knew her needs.

Some of Darla's friends drifted away due to busy lives, and some from fear. Even though they didn't like it, fear took over. Cancer was a scary word, a scary idea. They avoided her because they didn't know what to say and also because her illness was a reminder that something could happen to them. The isolation hurt Darla. Children don't realize the importance of presence. Many adults don't. I understood that other kids were afraid. It's natural. I didn't feel particularly brave, but I loved her and needed to help. After all, I could play games. And once we got used to the new situation, the illness often took a backseat to our play. She was simply my friend again. We forgot the illness and did all she could do and were even allowed to play with the makeup! There were times when Darla felt better and we could walk, swim, and ride bikes. Physical activity calms the mind and is good for anxiety and sadness. It is good for the body overall. We got out into the sun whenever we could. It brightened her mood.

It was great being with Darla and I wanted to be there often, but my mother made a point of making me stay involved with my other friends and activities. She said, "You can't go every day. You need to live your life. It's sad for her and nice of you, but you need your other friends and exercise. You need a balance." At the time it irritated me since she was the one who instilled in me the goodness of helping others, but I was thankful for her wisdom since it was healthier for me not to be totally immersed. I probably wouldn't have been as good for Darla if I had always been there. Sometimes I felt guilty for having my activities, but Darla wanted me to be happy and active. She did her homeschooling and had church activities. It was good for us to do some things separately. It gave us more to talk about. I was happy to hear about her days. She couldn't wait to hear funny stories about school. She wanted to hear about everything. I felt strange telling her about school and the other kids. Would she feel left out or get upset? Maybe she did, but she still wanted and needed to hear about them. We still wanted to talk about middle school, too, because soon she would be well and with us there! Hope and optimism play a key role in people feeling better and healing. We were very optimistic.

One of Darla's activities during this time was decorating her bedroom. She even had her own small black and white television, a birthday gift I envied! She got her own room when her sister got married and moved out. It was bittersweet as she missed Doris June, but she was thrilled to be able to make this room her own. A nice addition was a wall shelf for her cherished miniature horses. There were many types and they looked realistic. They were all lined up and on display. We no longer galloped them across the room. Darla's favorite was still the caramel brown, like her Pepe. She was surrounded by many of the things she loved, including a nice wooden cross on the wall over her bed. The room was blue and white with a beautiful canopy bed. If she had to be in bed often, she would do it in style, in a room fit for a princess! She adored her fancy bed. I did, too. It was quite nice to be in it, just hanging out talking or spending the night. The bright sunlight would come in through the pretty fabric, glittering and creating a fairyland. It was a very beautiful and comforting refuge.

Another activity involved her other birthday gift, an instant camera. It was very cool. It could pop out pictures seconds after they were taken! No waiting days for the film to be developed. You put in a film pack and, as the pictures were taken, they would magically slide out the slot—immediately. Nothing much seemed instantaneous in the 1960s so this was fascinating. It made for a great game or just an easy way to capture a memory. We couldn't go totally crazy with it. Unlike digital photos now, there was no deleting and trying again. Once the film pack was used, we had to beg for another. Still, it was fantastic.

SAD NEWS

After our adjustment to her illness, there came another major change. My dear friend had to have her leg amputated. They would take off the diseased part of her so her body could heal. Whoa. It's really hard for a kid to absorb that—hard for anyone. I can't imagine what Darla thought, waking up after surgery with only one leg. Overwhelming emotions: disbelief, anger, grief … all tangled together in a big mess. What??? How can I stand? How can I run? How can it hurt? On top of the emotional pain, there was physical pain. Some of her pain, phantom pain, was just plain strange.

Phantom pain is an interesting phenomenon. I was shocked and confused. How could her leg hurt when it wasn't there? How could her leg be itchy? Did her brain and nerves think her leg was still there? The sensations were still there. At first, it sounded kind of funny. I thought, *Wow, how weird is that? The leg is gone but it itches. Ha-ha.* But then it started sinking in that it was a real problem. The range ran from irritating to very painful. It was awful. They didn't know how to help her. Today more is known, but it seems that phantom pain is still not totally understood. Why did her leg hurt? Many treatments and medicines can now be used to help, including mirror therapy. In mirror therapy, the brain thinks the missing leg is there by seeing the reflection of the other, intact leg. When the intact leg is scratched, the brain thinks the missing leg has been scratched. Very clever. It was frustrating not to have a solution for Darla back then. Imagine having an itch that you can't scratch. Try it sometime. See how long you can take it. Darla had complex pain and complex emotions.

Emotions are often difficult to manage. We have emotions whether we like them or not. No feelings are bad. What we do with our emotions is what matters. Understandably, Darla had sadness and fear. She usually coped well, but fear can become too much and can turn into anger, which can be easier to express. For a while, she was acting mean, pushing me away. That hurt deeply. I tried to be patient and not take it personally. I knew I wasn't the enemy. It was the situation, fear and pain. Severe pain can take over your life—a focal point that saps all of your energy for anything else. It can pull you in and down quickly. She had to get through it. Her physical pain mixed with strong emotions was just overwhelming for a time. I understood that she was having pain and emotional issues but I couldn't understand the severity until I recently had a terrible accident. The pain was devastating and it was hard to think of anything else. Any movement shot daggers of pain through me. It zapped all energy. I couldn't even lie down. I slept in a recliner. It was all I could do to just sit and get through the days. Fortunately, my pain lasted only a few months, but I can better understand how poorly Darla felt at times. I'm surprised she only pushed me away once in the years she was ill.

I don't know if she had a support group as they have now but it might have helped her to talk with others going through similar situations; people who better understood her feelings. They could have understood each other's lives and perhaps been more open in discussing things. I hope Darla had someone to talk to, maybe another child who lost a limb or was going through cancer treatments. It's easy for most of us to think we know how someone feels. Perhaps we know that a lost leg changes things but do we truly understand how it affects them, how it feels? Of course, two people who have each lost a leg will have different feelings, but they certainly understand each other better than someone who has not gone through an amputation.

Eventually, poor Darla got through that hard time and went back to being her sweet self. Maybe she got new pain medicine. Maybe she had a good counselor and she got help and advice on coping with those negative feelings. Whatever it was, she was able to act differently. I am so glad she could do that so we could be together again. We were lonely. We both needed to be together, connected.

BLESSINGS

Mr. Spencer, our fifth-grade teacher, stayed connected to Darla and became a very good friend to her family. Maybe this was one of the reasons we were given that male teacher. He was such a blessing, visiting often. He had a calming presence, helping both Darla and her hurting family. He had worked with a chaplain in the army and was a great listener. He was very caring and helpful.

Darla's dog was another blessing to her, an emotional support dog. Her grandparents raised poodles and her father took her to choose her tiny Petie, a teacup poodle. How Petie got his name is disputed. Dianna says it's short for La Petite. He certainly was petite! I believe that he was named for Darla's favorite Monkee band member, Peter. Maybe it was a mixture of the two. Petie became white as he got older, losing the beautiful apricot color from when he was young. He was so darling, just a handful of pleasure. Sometimes he was used like a doll. With our help, he would be a circus dog, walking on his hind legs and clapping his front paws or flying through the air. He didn't feel mistreated. He loved the attention! When Darla would hop over and plop down on the couch, Petie would be ready to be held. He quickly learned how to jump up and sit so he wouldn't cause her pain. When he tired of being held, he'd bounce down and dance across the floor. When young, he would sometimes run so fast he'd slide across the floor, bump into something, and roll. Yelping, he sounded like a toy. Sometimes we'd roll around the floor with him, laughing hysterically. I had never imagined such a delightful creature! Petie was a great friend to Darla and a great diversion. He would nestle in her arms when she felt ill. He would be very calm when Darla pressed her face into his soft, curly fur. He snuggled right back into her. As with her pony, she and her pup had a special bond. He knew she needed him. He knew when to be a crazy and funny ball of energy, running in circles, and when to be cuddly and sweet, snuggled like a baby. I imagine he knew all of Darla's secret thoughts and feelings, whispered into his ear. He was a definite "up" in a time of extreme ups and downs.

Dealing with Misfortune

When going through an illness, both the sick person and others go through many emotions. Relationship dynamics can change. The other kids in a family get less attention from their parents when much time is spent on care and at doctors' offices and hospitals. Siblings might be angry, sad, fearful, or lonely. The family and friends go through confusion, grief, fear, and sadness. Sometimes it felt like forever before test results came back, creating tension as well. I didn't really understand emotions. It was hard. Everyone just did their best to handle them. I was very thankful that I could talk with my father. It was nice to have an empathetic listener. My mother was there and answered questions but she didn't want to talk much about Darla's illness. Due to my oldest sister's death from cancer when she was only four, Mom wanted to close off those feelings. My father didn't talk much, as it made him remember my sister, but he let me vent. Not everyone has someone to talk to in challenging times. I was blessed.

Dianna later told me she had been lonely. Her mother and Darla were often at the hospital, once for six weeks straight. Six weeks was a very long time for Darla to sit in a hospital bed and for Dianna to be so often without her mother. Dianna had to grow up quickly and take care of many of her own needs. It was hard for her. It was harder for all of the family. Even then, I understood, as well as a twelve-year-old could, that their mom wasn't a superwoman who could be in two places at once. Ruth wanted to be available for everyone's needs, but couldn't. I thought she was pretty superhuman to hold up so well. She always made things nicer with her incredible patience and big smiles! I can still see those great smiles when I think of her. Often, when the sick person gets attention, their caregivers can be overlooked. The fatigue from giving non-stop care can be overwhelming, leading to physical and emotional exhaustion. Hearing a sweet child desperately crying, "Mommy, it hurts," over and over and not being able to help is gut-wrenching. Being awake during long nights can create numbing fatigue. Sometimes the caregivers are so overwhelmed they get sick themselves. Respite and nurturing are crucial! Ruth needed nurturing. My mother was kind and caring, and wanted to be there for Ruth, and she often was, but it hurt her to be with Darla and Ruth because it reminded her of being with her own little girl. They were very good friends, but my mom had to have some distance sometimes. I hope Ruth got all the support and love she needed. She was such a great person. I heard she still got to hockey games on occasion. Other neighbors and family were of help and comfort as well. I was happy about that!

Love and patience are vitally important when difficult decisions must be made. Poor Ruth was miserable to have to tell her young daughter that her leg would be gone. She simply couldn't do it. The nurses had to help her. The hospital staff was nearly like family. They cared for Darla and her family physically, but also mentally and emotionally. They were wonderfully caring and compassionate. I worked at the same hospital several years after Darla was there and the staff remembered her well. They talked about Darla's sweetness and courage as well as how distressing it was for them. Nurses truly have my admiration, especially pediatric nurses. It takes special people to do this work. While working at that and other hospitals, I found that sometimes it took very little extra care to calm patients and make them happier. Once a nice lady was very anxious about her upcoming surgery and she disliked the television. During our short conversation, she mentioned she enjoyed music. A bit later, I was writing in my office and leaned over to turn on my transistor radio. *Bingo,* I thought. I took the radio to her room for her to use as a distraction until she was discharged. She was thrilled! It was amazing how much this small thing calmed her. In retrospect, perhaps it also made her feel good to have someone look at her as a person, not a patient. Sometimes hospitals can be so busy that the personal factor can be overlooked. Another woman was so grateful for a small kindness that her family brought me some cards of her own paintings. I was delighted that I could do little things that could make such a big difference to people. It all starts with compassion. I fully realized then, from my experiences, just how much the loving nurses supported Darla and her family!

I found it interesting when my doctor recently told me that, as part of their training, they had to be in various situations that mimicked patients' disorders so they would be more empathetic. They breathed through a straw to mimic lung problems, put petroleum jelly on glasses to mimic blindness, used a wheelchair around the hospital to encounter the challenges, had sleep deprivation to feel fatigued, etc. Maybe we should all try these things. We might be more patient. I've heard doctors say they were more empathetic after they had issues themselves, an accident or a serious illness. Sympathy, feeling sorry for someone, is good. However, empathy is a step further in relating to a person. It is connecting, having an understanding of what the other person is feeling. Greater understanding enhances care.

Not So Scary
After All

I remember walking down the hall of the hospital to visit Darla after her leg had been removed. My mother and I had waited a day or two before seeing her so she could heal a bit and get over some of the shock. I was very uncomfortable, literally shaking. Do we talk about her leg? Do we ignore it? We had been to the hospital before but now everything seemed awkward. Unknown territory. Our footsteps were too loud. The walls were too white. The smells of medicine and cleaning supplies made me sick. My stomach was upset. My heart was racing. When we quietly walked into her room, I couldn't speak. I tried to smile but my mouth wouldn't work. My smile was weird. She couldn't look at me anyway so I let the forced smile fall into an expression of concern. My fears for her swirled around me, not wanting to land. My mind raced and I wondered, *What should I do?* After a while, her eyes slowly slid toward me. Looking at her lovely face, I could see that she was overwhelmed and not really comprehending this huge change for her. She looked very small in that big hospital bed. She was extremely pale and her soft blue eyes blinked as though she hoped to wake up from a bad dream. Her trauma was obvious.

The sadness and fear showed, more than I wanted to see. I longed to comfort her. I desperately wanted to say, "It will be okay," but how could I? Valiantly trying to hold back tears, I summoned my courage. I took a deep breath and slowly walked up to her to tentatively touch her hand. "Sorry," came out as a croak. One small teardrop escaped, sliding down her beautiful face. Suddenly, we were weeping together—big, sad tears of anguish. Some people have certain people with whom they can be their true selves. I was one of Darla's people and glad of it. Being stoic is only good when necessary. She was a brave girl, but nobody should have to be brave all the time. Crying relieves stress. No regrets for crying. We let out all we could.

Nobody wanted to talk about her lost leg. It was on everyone's mind. I didn't want to look at her legs either, but my curiosity was strong. Unfortunately, while walking to a chair, I looked. I glimpsed a leg and a lump of a quarter of a leg under the sheet and looked away. My young mind had a hard time with the reality. Then I found myself staring. It was really … gone. Feeling out of control again, I thought to myself, *Stop! You can do this.* Flustered and not knowing what to say, I quietly sat by Darla while our mothers nervously chatted across the room, giving us time to reconnect. For several moments, we glanced at each other and looked away with a shyness, as if we were first meeting. Then a thought came to me. Was I looking at Darla's body or at Darla? With fresh understanding, I looked at *her* and it was okay. Not so scary. It was my turn to give her the gift of acceptance, no matter what she faced. She was still my friend, with a difference. A missing leg—a small change overall. When we think with our hearts, small differences are nothing. Our hearts know better. I smiled at her and she gave a tiny smile back. The ice was broken. We finally talked normally and then hugged goodbye saying, "See you soon!" I didn't like to see her suffering but left the hospital feeling happier. We could still be close. We could play like always, almost. We had hope that her body could now be well. Hope is a wonderful thing and it kept Darla moving forward through this tough time. And move forward she did.

Darla could have been stuck in bed after the amputation. After all, the loss of her leg was a loss of freedom—physical and, to some, mental. Some will feel uncomfortable and stay in. Not Darla! When trauma like this happens, there are choices. Does this break you or make you stronger? Does it stop you from truly living or do you take hold of the challenge and fight to be better? She would never be exactly as she was, just a bit different. Would that stop Darla? She made her choice. She was lively and was not going to sit. She didn't see her missing leg as a problem but as a challenge, and she was going to meet and conquer this challenge. She had a difference that didn't define her or change her daring spirit. It is in hardship and struggles that we discover aspects of our deeper selves. We find inner strength we didn't know we had. She was going to use that strength to do her very best. Her loving family had given her confidence and her feisty spirit drove her on.

There are some great movies and books that depict the lives of people with differences. They are very emotional pieces showing some of the difficulties people face daily. There can be emotional and physical pain, scars inside and out. The separation from others, seen in some stories, is heartbreaking. Though many stories begin by showing heartbreak, they can be uplifting—showing love and acceptance, through understanding. One such movie is *Wonder*. It is a story of a boy who has facial deformities. He needed multiple facial surgeries and wore a helmet outside his home to hide his face. He went to school for the first time, entering the fifth grade. It was a rough beginning as he struggled to be accepted, but ended nicely, with kids ignoring his difference and befriending him. He went from hiding to living freely. It was not easy to open up but so worth it. Such an inspirational story!

Much has been written and performed to portray the life of Joseph Merrick, also called John. *The Elephant Man* is a powerful biographical movie about a severely deformed man. His head was very large and deformed. His body was twisted, with one side enlarged. He was incredibly misshapen and lumpy. He couldn't even lie down to sleep. His mother died when he was a boy and he was poorly treated. Due to his deformities, his speech was difficult to understand and he had physical disabilities. He was shunned and had difficulties finding work. As depicted in the movie, he ended up in shows where he was displayed as a "curiosity." People would often taunt and laugh at him, or scream. His owner spoke of him as "it" and kept him like a caged animal. He was hurt physically and emotionally. Eventually, it took only a few people to look at him kindly and help to change his life altogether. A surgeon heard of him and became a friend. He arranged for him to live in the London Hospital where he was at first greatly feared but was later better understood. Most people then treated him very well. He began to have visitors who helped him feel accepted and confident. They took him out in public so people could become comfortable with him. He beamed with joy at the theater. As people got to know this gentle person, they realized that he was quite refined and intelligent, with a good, kind soul. His prized possession, his only possession for most of his life, was a picture of his dear mother. Sometimes his eyes, barely seen due to disfigurement, grew meltingly soft to match his gentle voice. For being treated so well, his gratitude was so profound he could hardly express the depth of it. Between his breaks to suck in drool, he murmured his thanks with intensity. Someone cared. Someone cared about him. He wept at the realization of having friends. He was an intelligent, talented, and loving man who had severe medical conditions that made him look very different from others and contributed to much of his life being one of torment. His last years were his happiest since his time with his mother, yet they were still marred by some terrible treatment by some who couldn't see his true being. Everybody deserves love. Every body deserves love. How can people be so cruel to nice, gentle people? How can we change it?

Unfortunately, many people do make judgments of character based on looks, and then treat people according to their judgments. What a terrible mistake. If we see beyond looks to discover the soul of a person, perhaps we'll find a wonderful friend. Maybe if we see with our hearts there can be progress and hope for better lives for everyone—those with differences as well as those who are growing by learning to accept and appreciate those who look different.

There are many sad stories about people, real and fictional, who have hidden themselves away for years, sometimes decades. Mary Balogh wrote a touching story about a woman who stayed hidden due to a large purple birthmark on her face. She was miserable, yet felt she had no choice but to stay hidden, trapped due to her fear of ridicule. Maybe people feel as though they have protection in their cocoons, but they can feel imprisoned. Perhaps when one feels unwanted, they make themselves disappear. In that way, they feel in control—in control yet imprisoned. Someone gradually drew out this lovely person and she began to enjoy living a normal life. In fact, she was thrilled to expand her life, experiencing things she'd never allowed herself to do. She was freed from her own limitations, her own restrictions. Some still looked at her oddly but she realized that after a time, people became accustomed to her face and ignored the mark. She found that if she didn't act uncomfortable about it, others weren't long uncomfortable. Sometimes people were curious enough to ask about it. She simply and cheerfully answered any questions and went on living in joy, feeling very thankful to have found the courage to venture out. Fears are often our own thoughts, with little foundation. Yes, she had a face that was different from most faces, but she expected people to shun her without knowing if the shunning would actually happen. Her thoughts didn't usually match reality. News stories tell of people who expected to hear negative comments when first showing their differences. They were surprised when others didn't really care or they got a positive response instead. How wonderful it is when fear can be forgotten and a person can live joyfully.

There are many great books and movies about animals with differences. From a fictional dragon with a prosthetic tail fin to a real dolphin with a prosthetic tail, creatures with differences abound in both fictional and real-life stories. The movie *Dolphin Tale* is about Winter, a bottlenose dolphin who was caught in a crab trap. She lost her tail when the rope cut off her circulation. She was rescued and taken to an aquarium in Florida where they nursed her back to health, including getting a prosthetic tail for her. She swam awkwardly before getting her new tail. The prosthetic was tricky to make because she also lost a joint needed for some movements. However, an intelligent and creative team designed a prosthetic tail as well as a special liner to go between her body and tail. The liner was for comfort and stability and is now used for human amputees. Many kids with disabilities, some with their own prosthetic limbs, related to Winter. Some connected through the movie and some got to visit her in Florida, getting to pet her and watch her play in her fancy new tail. She was a great inspiration! When she recently died after sixteen years, many were saddened, including all the people she inspired to be positive about their physical issues and special bodies.

Some pets have only two or three instead of four legs. They are just the same inside and just as lovable. I have seen some dogs and cats with missing legs and they get along wonderfully, trotting down the street quite happily. My neighbor had a nice little dog that had a little cart with wheels because his back legs didn't work well. He loved getting out for a walk. My friend has a dog with no eyes. She says he's the sweetest dog ever. How cool does a lizard with two tails sound? How about a cat with two faces? It is a real thing and is very cute. One of these Janus cats lived a long life. My friends have a tortoise that lost a leg. They glued on a wheel for him to get around more easily. The Maryland Zoo has a box turtle with a Lego wheelchair! People find these creatures interesting and even amusing. Are people with missing body parts treated like this? We obviously don't want to laugh at people and their new devices, but it's easier to be accepting if we are at ease and comfortable talking with them, assuming they are open to talking about their differences. Asking respectfully is pivotal. Many welcome a chance to show who they truly are, instead of being the person with a difference.

My father was a people watcher. A favorite spot to do it was at an outdoor market. He loved to see differences. Sometimes we would see something we had never seen before, a look or action, and sometimes we would be surprised by something we wouldn't have expected from that particular person. I appreciate the differences in people from being with Dad. One of my favorite movie scenes is in *Star Wars*, the cantina. All of the characters look wildly different—human, animal, and other creative beings. It's so much fun to see such an assortment of characters! I went to a festival recently and just wandered, watching people. Little kids played together, accepting all, seeing no differences in each other. There were all sorts of styles and colors in clothes and hair in addition to the people themselves. One man had prosthetic legs that looked tanned and shaped to look very muscular. Another had a metal leg. I enjoyed watching a dancer in a wheelchair whirl around enthusiastically. Life is so rich when we are not exactly the same.

A New Leg

Darla was soon going to get her new leg. Wow! This was something I had never seen, a prosthetic limb. It was an interesting concept. Another ray of hope. With a new leg, she would be able to do much more. But first things first. A small part of her leg, the stump, was left so that it would fit into her new leg. At first, the stump was swollen and the end was ugly—red and puckered, with wide black stitches like movie monsters. Though I tried not to show it, I did recoil at first, just as I would when seeing any wound. To be told about it and to see it were two different things! During these times, I found I had strength, too. I could handle more than I expected. Her stump had to heal before the prosthetic leg could be used. For weeks, the stump was cleaned and rewrapped with gauze, like a mummy. We could be grossed out and refuse to look or we could deal with it with humor. We chose humor. She had to deal with it, might as well laugh about it. It was interesting—what could be horrifying to some could be amusing to two young kids. Sometimes we broke out in giggles. It sounds crazy when thinking of what that stump was and represented, but the best way we could accept it was with humor, so "the monster" it was. During a severe illness or trauma, the sweet sound of laughter is music to the soul.

Eventually, the stump was healed, with a healthy pink scar, and Darla could get her new leg. We were very excited and somewhat nervous. Finally, the day came when her prosthetic leg was ready. It was made of tan hard plastic and wood, and surprisingly heavy. It bent at the knee but didn't move otherwise, no ankle or side-to-side movement. She paused and took in a deep breath, as if to draw in courage. She nodded to her helpers. With a look of concentration and determination, she slowly stood up and gripped the handrails. At the first step, she grunted as her stump sat deeper into the leg. With a grimace, another step. She hissed as she let out a breath. Each step was a struggle. Her eyes were glistening with tears. It was awkward and it hurt both her stump and her tiny waist, where the belt pushed. Like her family, I wished I could take on some of the pain and lessen it for her. She sat down with her shoulders slumped. Poor Darla! This was not only painful but also very disappointing as we thought she might learn to walk somewhat normally, maybe even dance. Those dreams were gone, at least for the near future. Maybe later, when she was stronger or bigger? She really tried to use her new leg, but it was difficult for her. But wait, regroup. This is an adventurer here. Depression and sadness have a place but they can also waste time and energy. She gave them a short time and then moved on. She was determined to live her best life. She moved forward with gusto.

Darla decided that she would wear the heavy, hard leg only when she had to. Some people with amputations choose not to use prosthetics and that's okay. She could still easily get around with crutches or hopping, her usual method around home or in and out of the wheelchair. At first, her dogs were curious and somewhat alarmed at her hopping, staying a good distance from her. They watched a while and, after a short initial curiosity and like most people, they accepted it and calmed down. Darla used a wheelchair when out for a long time, like at the zoo or on a shopping trip. She looked quite small in that big wheelchair. A tiny girl with a big heart!

Darla's artificial leg was heavy and painful, but now there are great prosthetic legs. Some are made to look very natural and some are made with metal, designed for function. People can jump and run with some of them. Watch people in the Paralympics and other programs. With some adaptations, special running blades for example, people with disabilities can use and show their athletic skills. It's great to see few, if any, limitations. When I think of Darla's clunky leg of the 1960s, I am amazed by the wonderful new prosthetics. I applaud the clever designers and creators as well as the terrific athletes using the prosthetics.

Apparently, it is now possible for some people to move prosthetic body parts with their thoughts, the way our brains normally work with body parts. This is a fantastic field that continues to progress. Maybe someday we will learn how to grow back appendages like some lizards regrow tails. For now, there are prosthetics that function quite well.

So many things are available and being created to make life easier for people with disabilities—crosswalks with sounds and ramps, elevators, signs in Braille, swimming pool chairs to lower people into the water, chairs to go up staircases, electronic voice devices, wheelchair vans, audiobooks, hearing aids, adaptive devices and clothing, etc. There are clothing lines with magnets, Velcro, or snaps as well as different styling like flaps. These make dressing much more manageable for some people. Other items simply make life more fun. People have designed adaptive machines including tricycles with hand pedals for wheelchair users and tandem bikes with wheelchairs for those who need to stay in their chairs. I was recently introduced to sled ice hockey, another way for people with disabilities to enjoy sports. Some can propel themselves on their sleds and some are helped by pushers. I especially enjoy the little kids' games. I can easily imagine Darla on a sled, sliding around the ice rink, her hockey stick moving toward the puck. She would have the widest smile!

Respect for Others

At first, Darla was a bit hesitant to go out in public, but my fearless friend went out regularly. I remember a day at the grocery store when Darla was using the wheelchair. Sometimes she wore her prosthetic leg in the chair, but when it hurt too much, she wouldn't wear it. Sometimes her comfort was more important than what people would think of her missing leg. Either way, she was in a wheelchair and so she didn't look as expected. Many kids would try to come up and talk to her. Parents would pull them back in embarrassment. I wondered about this. By now, her missing leg was normal to me. The wheelchair was normal. Why couldn't kids be with her and talk to her? They were just curious, as I had been. I could imagine them wanting to ask, "What happened to your leg?" or "Why are you in a wheelchair? Is it fun?" Simple questions that I thought should be answered. Not a long answer, just something quick like, "My leg was sick." Some people could simply say, "I was born this way." Sometimes kids are better at accepting reality than adults. Wouldn't they rather get an answer and then continue talking to her than be scared of someone with one difference? Did they wonder why I could be with her and they couldn't? Some kids aren't easy with such things and parents can decide to keep them away.

I imagine that the frightened children stayed away anyway. However, I think it would be better if adults give a gesture of comfort, and then assure kids that what may at first look odd is quite fine and not scary. Maybe then they wouldn't be afraid the next time someone looked different. Most kids were just curious. Darla wasn't so scary when she smiled and talked to them. Some people have just one leg. It's okay. It was normal for her. When they got to know the person inside the different body, they forgot about it or it was even cool, not just a boring body like everyone else's.

Of course, if she was sad or in pain, it was not the right time to talk to her about it. All they had to do was look at her. If she was sitting upright and smiling, she was ready to talk. If she looked sad or slumped over and she wasn't looking up, it wasn't a good time. It is important to consider any person's mood, but it is even more important with a person in Darla's situation. Sensitivity to feelings is key. Asking "Is this a good time for you to talk?" or "Would you mind sharing?" or "Hi. May I sit with you?" would be polite starts.

Sometimes people would see that she was missing a leg and it would be frightening or even funny to them. They would make faces. I understood, since I winced when first seeing Darla's stump, but I wished people would turn away when they made faces or laughed. It wasn't good for her to see them. I remember seeing people walk way around Darla to avoid her. Some stared. Sometimes when walking into a place, it became very quiet. At times, kids would point and snicker or make rude comments. To be teased or ignored hurt her. They were wounding her, even if it didn't show. I would become frustrated, sad, and angry—for her. I didn't want to be mean or rude back, though I admit it was tempting. I just wanted to shout, "She's Darla and she's a great person. Be nice! Treat her like any other kid!" How could we get through to them? Curiosity can be solved fairly easily. Communication and education can combat fear and might at least lessen unintentional grimacing and such. How do we get through to those who don't seem to care?

Consider the scenario of this sweet little girl who is nervous but brave enough to venture out. Her leg is gone. Not only does she have to cope with physical pain, but also emotions that most of us can't imagine. She is only twelve. She has tried to be nice and outgoing, leaving the shelter of her home. She just needs understanding. Most of the time, she gets that understanding, but some people are rude and hurtful. Words can harm, a lot. Actions like teasing or avoiding can hurt. Some people act poorly out of ignorance. Some don't really think about the other person. People are ignoring her or even laughing. Words can hurt terribly or words can really help. Which would you want to give to Darla? I hope kind, inclusive words. Acceptance and inclusion are important to someone with a difference. Just a smile could help. Once people get used to a difference, it's not scary at all. It's fine. We need to be open and acknowledge everyone. The first step may be to realize that we are fearful and ask ourselves why. Can we imagine this person with a disability as a friend or relative? They are someone's friend or relative. Would we be fearful if we ate dinner with them every night? Of course not. We would be very comfortable. It doesn't matter if someone looks different from society's norms. Everybody deserves respect and kindness.

People with disabilities and differences can approach the world in many ways and their approach may change. Darla was often fine knowing that some people acted strangely with her. Yet some days, it bothered her. Some people are very independent and don't need or want help. They are happy to go about enjoying life, ignoring their difference. Some hide or build defenses to avoid being hurt. If someone has been treated poorly, it's quite understandable that they would build walls, so to speak, to protect themselves. The heart can sometimes only take so much. Walls may ward off some pain but they can also diminish life and increase other types of pain. Some people become angry and lash out. This may be understandable but not ideal. Perhaps some of these people could be coaxed out and changed if they had some people who treated them well.

I was proud of Darla. She bravely went out and welcomed people. She was accepting of her difference and she was open and kind. Sometimes we would laugh when we saw a kid being hauled away from her. We understood that the parent was just nervous. Still, it was sad that she couldn't talk with them. The children may have thought she was separated from them because of her small difference. Adult fear kept the children from meeting a wonderful person. Due to their fear, the adults missed a chance to teach their children acceptance. She was the same nice and fun person that she had been with two legs. She still loved her pony, her dogs, and playing. The other kids would have benefited from realizing that she really hadn't changed.

As much as Darla could do many things, we were aware that she had to be left out of some things. For example, it was a big deal that the training camp for the Arizona State University football team was open to kids for summer camp. One summer, I was very excited because I was able to go with other friends to Camp Tontozona. It was beautiful—a cool, wooded area with a natural rock swimming hole! We got to do all the typical camp things like crafts and outings, including hiking to the swimming area. There were crackling campfires where we sang and heard stories while eating tasty snacks like s'mores. Darla could only hear about our adventure. I was open but cautious as I told her about it. Even though she didn't show envy, I felt sorry for her. It had to be difficult for her to stay home. All the more reason to include her in things she could do!

Good News at Last

We went about our lives as usual. We continued swimming, riding, playing, and eating our favorite foods. We also visited the zoo often to see the animals she was drawn to, her friends. We all assumed she would work in a field with animals, maybe at the zoo!

During this time, Darla was tested to follow her progress—to see if the cancer was gone. This caused some anxiety, but we learned to compartmentalize it. We just ignored it whenever possible. It sat in the back of our minds while we waited for results. The test after her amputation was … good news! She was free from cancer. Elation! Everyone was so happy to hear that she was in remission! The cancer was gone. She was healthy again! Relief flooded in. A bit of concern lingered but joy totally eclipsed any other emotion. It was an emotional renewal. Remission is wonderful. Life is so precious, it is to be lived to the fullest!

We often take our health and bodies for granted, especially before losing any function or having pain. Bodies are complex and intricate machines beyond comprehension for most of us. It's hard to believe so much goes on inside us! Remission from cancer was a great time to remind us to appreciate our bodies and take good care of them. We much appreciated that Darla was feeling good and getting around again.

Darla was able to go to seventh grade and reunite with friends. She was very happy! She would be in middle school, just as we had imagined. Ruth took her to school since she couldn't easily get on the bus and she needed her wheelchair. Sometimes I got to ride with them. Ruth also took us to many school sporting events. We had to wear dresses to school back then so Darla's prosthetic leg showed. Luckily, fishnet stockings were in and they covered her leg fairly well. Of course, it was still obvious when she walked. The leg was clunky so she only took a few steps to transfer, mostly to and from her wheelchair. The first day, she was both excited and nervous, a rare thing for my fearless friend. I could tell she was nervous by her facial expression. She stopped briefly and collected herself, took a deep breath, and said, "Let's go!" And off she went. Little shoulders back and her head held high, she held herself with dignity. She was brave. The kids stared at first, some with looks of pity (which she didn't like) and many with curiosity. Overall, people adjusted pretty well. She was eventually known and didn't feel like a spectacle. She had old grade-school friends who more quickly accepted her difference. Unfortunately, some were still ill at ease. They were unsure how to talk with her. Again, I wanted to say, "Treat her like anyone else!" Actually, sometimes I would say it and remind them that they didn't have to talk about her illness or amputation. Darla preferred to talk about current happenings. She was so appreciative of her good health, her precious remission!

Strangely, I don't remember being at lunch with Darla. Maybe our schedules didn't work out. I hope people asked her to eat with them. I hope people smiled and talked with her. Even her old friends could be uncomfortable, I knew. I hoped they would overcome their fears and jump into inviting her to sit with them. If anyone thought she wouldn't have much to say, that she must be sad or unable to do much, they were wrong. She was active and didn't let her missing leg stop her. She rode her beloved pony with the help of her father's clever strap to keep her prosthetic leg in the stirrup. She rode her bike with a similar device from her father, a pedal that allowed her to lift up as well as push down. She cared for her animals. She often swam in her neighbor's backyard pool. No need for two legs in a pool, Darla swam like a fish! A fish uses two fins and a tail, similar to what Darla had. She had always been a good swimmer and was still good! She liked to hop up onto the diving board to show her talent. She was much better at diving and swimming than I would ever be. I just had fun and that's what counted. We weren't competitive at all. Well, I take it back … she loved to win when playing cards.

Darla was a busy girl. She got involved with her church's girls' group since her religion was very important to her. Ruth took us to our school games and they also went to her brother Dennis's high school ball games. Darla also enjoyed watching the rides and playing games at Legend

City amusement park, where Dennis worked. While she couldn't experience every attraction, she loved the Sky Ride and could play some games. It was an exciting place with bright lights, rides, food, and games. It was fun just to be there and feel the excitement. Dennis called himself a ham. He loved to make people laugh, especially Darla. He was a natural to work there.

A wonderful new surfing "beach" was built in Tempe only a couple of miles from our homes. It was wild—surfing in the desert. Big Surf Waterpark had five-foot waves for surfers and three-foot waves for boogie boarding and play. My brother and his friends learned to surf there, so they were part of the entertainment. Big Surf had a concert area where many bands such as the *Beach Boys* and *Pink Floyd* played. It was so much fun! Ruth took us and we enjoyed watching the activities. Darla didn't go into the water. I'm sure it was hard for her to sit out, but she was happy to experience the incredible place, this desert beach. The wheelchair couldn't get very close and crutches wouldn't work well, sinking into the sand unevenly. Luckily, Darla was light and could easily be carried to sit on a towel. She covered her legs with another towel so others weren't uncomfortable. A fun memory of that time was getting a hot pink bikini. Ruth took me to buy a bikini when a group of friends was going to Big Surf. She and Darla were very enthusiastic about the event and enjoyed helping me choose my swimsuit. It was fun for me because I felt special getting the attention and, also, I knew my mother would flip out when I came home with a bikini. Ruth was a happy and free spirit sort of person, despite what they were enduring. I connected with her because I felt like a free spirit myself. I just needed a nudge to let it out. We both enjoyed bright colors, hence the hot pink. Yes, my mother flipped out but, to my surprise, I got to keep the swimsuit. I felt sad that Darla wasn't able to go, especially since she had a crush on one of the guys going with us. However, she seemed happy for me and thoroughly enjoyed the shopping trip. Of course, afterward, they wanted a full report. It was amazing except that I got a horrible sunburn and was lobster red. They were caught between laughing at me and feeling sorry for me. It was before sunscreen was invented, so I knew I'd get an extremely painful burn after a multiple-hour event. It took two days of healing before I could go see them. It hurt, but boogie boarding in the desert? It was worth it!

Though we were still too young to date, we chattered about guys and dreamed of the day someone would ask us out. Where would we go and what would we do? Darla had already been waiting for three years. We just assumed that many guys could overlook Darla's missing leg and love her for her sweetness and fun personality. She would be a great date and a caring girlfriend.

Darla enjoyed all of nature and the Grand Canyon was one of her favorite places, a natural wonder of the world. A breathtaking view! It's hard to fully understand it except when seeing it in real life. Its splendor cannot be fully realized in a photo. In the 1960s, you could look at the canyon from above, hike down into the canyon, and raft the Colorado River at the bottom of the canyon. Now there are more tourist features including a zipline and a glass bridge jutting out seventy feet over the canyon. People can walk out over the rim of the canyon onto the clear glass horseshoe-shaped bridge and look down to the bottom of the canyon—Darla's type of thrill! To celebrate her remission and have a change of scenery, Ruth set up a trip to the south rim of the canyon for us. Dianna brought a friend and we all took the five-hour drive for an overnight trip in their camper. Luckily, the south rim area was set up for wheelchairs even in the 1960s. We could walk around and see the spectacular views—white billowy clouds sliding across the vivid blue sky above and the beautiful layers of colored rock below. We stood quietly, staring at the large expanse and listening to the wind playing with the bushes. I heard Darla sigh as if this were the best thing she'd ever seen! We watched the clouds and discussed what shapes we thought they made. We watched as the clouds made shadows on the rock walls below, briefly darkening their colors. The high point of the day was the brilliant sunset. At night, due to the lack of city lights, there was a spectacular show of stars. We could see so many stars, in layers, like a scarf I once had—silver sparkles in folds of rich dark chiffon. Beautiful. It was a great time. Everyone was so very happy that Darla was healthy and enjoying activities again!

A Sad Change

Many remissions are wonderful and permanent, with no recurrence. Unfortunately, Darla's remission was wonderful and short. It was an unbelievably great sorrow to find that her cancer had returned. One short sentence made me quiver—"It's back." Darla had more chemotherapy and radiation treatments, and surgery on her spine. Different emotions bubbled up: disbelief, despair, and even anger. The end of her remission seemed like falling into a pit. A huge letdown. We had to crawl out of that pit to get back on course. Eventually, renewed determination and hope made their way in. A renewal of positivity. It was hard to get to the same level of hope as before her remission but she did not give up. A couple of times, darkness overcame her. Worry and depression lurked. Who could help it? Yet, she would always pull out of it, rise up, and become stronger. Her strength won over the depression. I truly admired her courage and her determination to be positive.

There were still good days when she felt well enough to hang out and play and we took great advantage of those times. We did as many normal things as possible, making the most of our time. We still played silly games like hide-and-seek but played indoors. She just needed extra time to get into her hiding spot. I recall one frustrating time when I looked all over but I could not find that girl. I was almost ready to give up when giggles broke out and I followed them. Looking again in the closet, I could not see her. A muffled laugh made me look up. There she was scrunched up on the high shelf, with a wide grin telling me, "I gotcha!" Her long braid was wrapped over her. How in the world? She had help from her sneaky brother-in-law and sister, Moe and Doris June. They popped in and we all had a great laugh. Darla was still the instigator of crazy, fun times!

We would often sit on the same lounge chair and ponder life. Now our conversations were much deeper than if she had been well. We had more to consider than just the day-to-day matters of young teens. Life was definitely complex. The real issue of severe illness and how to best handle it were part of our discussions, but we also had some fun teen talks in that lounger. People have to deal with what they get. We would always think about how to make the best of life. What little trips could we do? When she felt like eating, we'd jump on making those sweet, gooey chocolate-chip cookies. Now she was allowed to eat a whole batch if she wanted, something our eight-year-old selves had begged to do.

Darla had multiple issues due to chemotherapy, like incredible exhaustion and gastrointestinal problems. She lost weight, and she had little to begin with. Her movement slowed. Sometimes she didn't even have the energy to open her eyes. It was heartbreaking to watch her change and to see her in pain. At some point, she moved from her lovely canopy bed to a hospital bed in her home. She became more dependent on help, often needing to be carried. We all felt helpless except to give her support. It was also hard to know exactly how to act. Situations and feelings often changed. To know how to best support her at any given time, I had to listen to her and follow her lead. We prayed and I helped with anything I could.

She tried everything possible to get better, but despite her valiant effort, during eighth grade, it was accepted that she would not improve. No more chemotherapy. No more tests. The goal changed to making her as comfortable as possible, just enjoying life and doing what she could. She was so sweet. Many of us might say, "Why me?" but Darla never seemed bitter or angry. During her long ordeal, she was somehow the same content soul she was when she was younger. She looked to God and received peace.

That peace was needed to come to acceptance. Sadly, she would not have her dreams. She wouldn't have her dates or even a first kiss. So … she decided to live those things through me. Feisty little Darla gave me a smile one day. Not a sweet one—one of those sly little grins that made me cringe. I lifted my eyebrows and stared, waiting for it. "Go find somebody to kiss you," she said quite nonchalantly. "Ha!" I squeaked, "I don't think it's that easy." "Well, it can be," she said, pretty sure of herself. I was willing to do an awful lot for her, but this? Yikes.

Unfortunately, I had already told her I liked someone. So it didn't come as a total surprise, but it certainly wasn't comfortable. Okay, maybe I could try to get to know him? Maybe I could give nature a little push, time-wise. And maybe, if he liked me, he'd be willing to kiss me. I gulped and conceded, "Tell you what, I won't go begging but I'll try and, if it happens, you'll be the first person I tell." Excited, she quickly plotted how I should go about this. After a couple of crazy ideas were quickly discarded, the plan turned out to be simple. I should just get over my fear, walk on up and say hello. She was hilariously pushy—and it worked. I kissed two guys in the latter part of eighth grade. One of them asked me to go steady. How exciting! It lasted a whole week. That made Darla chuckle. I'd gladly go through it again just to hear her chuckle. In fact, I did. The second relationship didn't last much longer. That time, I got a much heartier laugh as well as a bit of sympathy. I was glad I could share the experiences with her, short as they were. I told her that first kisses were awkward but nice. Holding hands was very nice. Being dumped, not so much. It's hard to put those feelings into words for someone, but I did my best. Darla loved sharing my thrills and embarrassments!

We laughed and we cried together. Sometimes she didn't want the negative emotions of others to sway her feelings so she had to close off. She didn't want to see others cry from sadness or see pity because she wanted to maintain her positivity. Understandable and commendable. She confided that nighttime was the hardest time for her, with fewer distractions and activities to keep her from thinking about the pain or fear that sometimes crept in. I was glad she had her family and her dog. Petie was always cuddled with her at night. That is likely when he heard her deepest feelings and thoughts, whispered in his ear. We tried to be positive, creating good times. We ignored her illness as much as we could and continued to do everyday things. She even kept up her studies, wanting to graduate from middle school with her friends. She had all the good traits of a warrior, my dear and feisty friend. She was strong and brave. I often wondered if I could be so brave. It's impossible to say. However, I was proud to be her friend. While some go bald during chemotherapy, Darla's hair grew long. To me, she looked like a lady warrior with her long braid, nearly to her waist.

Darla's recurring illness and decline were extremely sad to watch but it was also an extraordinary experience—seeing great strength, faith, and courage in a young girl. She had bad days filled with pain yet she wrote in a diary how very glad she was to be able to live each new day. Darla thanked God for her family, including her beloved little niece, her sister's first child. Doris June and Moe lived in a different Arizona city but visited often with their precious daughter. As babies often are, Kathie was a very bright light in Darla's life. She so looked forward to their visits. Who wouldn't be happier snuggled up to a sweet little baby? Darla would press her lips to that soft tiny head and Kathie would tilt to gaze up at her adoring aunt. They had tender, loving smiles! Each day, Darla gave thanks for all she had.

JOY

Darla's joy of life was amazing. She cared about other people, not focusing on her illness. She transcended the negative and looked to the good in life. She had a positive view of life just as it was, just as she was. Was she sad that she couldn't swim at Big Surf or go to dances? I never saw any negativity. Dianna believes she was happy just to hear about the adventures. Darla was selfless, loving, and sweet. She seemed to understand connection in a way that I am still learning. Her joy came from knowing that she was connected with God. It gave her peace. She knew the power of love was hers, simply for being aware and accepting it. Imagine life if we all understood and lived in the knowledge of connectedness. We are never alone and always loved. Imagine living with a great sense of peace, knowing all is well.

Darla taught us patience and to be grateful for the good we had in life. She used challenges as a time of spiritual growth and was thankful for them. I was amazed at the awareness she had. We were all so lucky to be part of her life. We grew from her growth. Her positive spirit radiated to us. I was glad for that because I needed it. I struggled. I tried not to show them, but I had bad feelings. Sometimes I got angry. My best friend was being taken away. She could do less and less. I couldn't help her, which made me feel helpless and sad. I was fearful of losing her. It was strange—I was also envious. She had this connectedness that I didn't. Though the rest of me was struggling, my heart was glad she had that true joy. I prayed that I could follow her to that state and told her so. She said, with a gentle smile, "You will grow in peace and love. Enjoy life."

Darla was also in a state of being in the present. She had no worries about her past or future. Living in the present opens us to enjoy the moment, what we have now. We should all learn from that. Slow down. Use all of your senses. See beauty. Look at the sky and ponder. Smell the earth and flowers. Truly feel animals' fur—and their love. Hear voices and music. Take time to taste your food. It's a wonderful way to live, simply to be. Darla saw beauty in life itself. She found joy in simple things—bright stars, cooing babies, loving animals, brilliant sunsets, clouds changing shapes, iridescent hummingbirds zipping by and sipping at beautiful flowers, and smiles. She seemed to love everyone. She was peaceful because of her belief that she was in God's hands. Her faith in the afterlife was strong. She was radiant. Her family called her an angel. Being with her was a joy because she was joyful!

Sometimes when she was lying still, eyes closed, I gazed at her—trying to store every detail in my memory. So still, I could almost see her floating on a sea of love, delicately held by God. Love itself held that sweet soul who was nearly ready to find her total peace. I dreaded losing her and yet I wanted peace for her. Her body was ill and she was in pain but her soul was not. Her soul was quite well and happy, waiting for her transition.

In the spring of eighth grade, I asked if I could have a party for Darla instead of my birthday party. It was very important to me. My mother agreed it would be a great way to honor her. The cancer had spread. Her time was short. I've always thought funerals were backward. If possible, a celebration of life should be with the celebrated person! Each person at the party told a funny or sweet story about being with Darla and she had to guess who it was. Her friend would then come out and give her a very careful hug, like an air hug. We ate cake and played some old-fashioned games that were easier for Darla, games such as "How many clothespins can you get into the bottle?" and "How many items can you remember on the tray?" We laughed that we were all better at clothespins when we were in third grade. Maybe we were more patient then? It was a bittersweet party. Seeing Darla so small and sick was difficult, especially for those who hadn't seen her for a long time, yet it was a light-hearted and special time with her. I was happy to see Darla with her friends and appreciated the ability to celebrate such a deserving person.

Darla was extremely proud and thankful that she got to finish eighth grade through homeschooling. She had worked hard for her achievement—middle school graduate! The superintendent and others held a special early graduation ceremony in her home. It was very touching.

A Passing

Just a month or so after our party, a good friend came to tell me Darla had peacefully passed away at her home. I held tightly to the doorknob to stay standing. I was in shock, totally overwhelmed. I couldn't process it. I had known this news was coming. I knew it was coming soon. Still, I stared at him, thinking he must be mistaken yet knowing he was not. He patiently waited. Often the brain negates something or will be silent, as if waiting for us to be ready to take in what we see or hear. Time seems to stand still or go in slow motion. It's normal but odd. I vaguely felt a hug. The touch slowly brought me to reality. My stiffness finally left and I sagged. I was glad to have my friend's support. When I finally accepted she was gone, I felt like I had a hole in my heart. A fog settled over me. I would never again be with Darla.

It was brave of my friend to do this difficult task and I thanked him for giving me the news so gently. Then I had to ask him to let me be alone. All I could do was sit in my loneliness and cry, hard. I sat on the edge of the footstool, curled up, my arms wrapped around myself, rocking and sobbing. My mind played through our time together. As I looked around, everything was the same, but nothing was the same. A piece of me was missing. The sobbing started anew. What would my life be without my soulmate? I wanted to grow old with her. I wanted to see her kids and watch her work with animals. I'd known that wasn't going to happen, but the reality hit hard. Our dreams were gone. She had gone to another place. I had only known her for half my life and, for nearly half of that time, she had been sick. How was that fair? I was crushed and dumbfounded. I wondered, *How did this happen? How do I go on alone?* I sat and stared at a wall, and cried.

Some people think crying doesn't help and some actually get angry, telling people to stop. I disagree. It is necessary to let grief out—emotionally, mentally, and physically. Tears can be healing. People need to be allowed to grieve in whatever way suits them, assuming nobody is hurt. Cry, talk it out, write it out, hug a person or an animal, yell, or beat on a pillow. Talk to school, church, or other professional counselors. Talk with kind, caring friends or close family members. Go to support groups with people who have been in similar situations. There are many ways to heal. We just need to let those feelings out in a good, healthy way. I used many of these sources at different times in my grieving process. I still do. The agony of loss is never completely gone but, as it is said, it can get easier with time and support.

The day after I got the sad news, some friends came over and we mourned together. We relived our wonderful party and talked about our remarkable friend who lived and died with such grace. Everyone around Darla had greatly grown from seeing her strength of character, courage, and positivity during her challenges. We could follow her example when we had our own challenges and help others with theirs.

We saw Darla once more—at her funeral. It, too, was bittersweet. I thought, *How can this be so devastating and uplifting at the same time?* When I thought of myself, it was painful to have to let her go. When I thought of Darla, it was good. It was healing to see my sweet friend look pain-free and totally at peace, with that beautiful soft smile. It was easy to envision her with God and her loved ones who had passed on. I knew that her loving spirit soared. That made me smile.

Life is ever-changing, like a kaleidoscope. You roll along and experience some bright wonderful things and also have some darker times. During our darker times, we looked towards the Light and things looked brighter. Darla was a pro at seeing the Light.

For a decade, Ruth kept her little girl's room as it was. She couldn't bear to dismantle it. All the memories were there, sweet and sad. I still have Darla's gold cross necklace. When I received that necklace, I carefully slid it through my fingers like a rare treasure. It is my earthly connection to her, surely a treasure. It gives me comfort to have her with me in that way.

Darla and I had a wonderful friendship and I remember her with much love. Sometimes I feel her spirit with me, love and peace surrounding me. I envision her with her mother now, riding ponies and giggling. Some day, I'll join them and we'll ride through the clouds.

LIFE LESSONS
FROM DARLA

Purpose

Darla was fearless, loving, and joyful! She lived and died with grace. Her short life was very important to many of us. She helped us open our hearts and minds and gave us unconditional love. Thank you, my friend!

Everyone is important to the world. We may not see this, because a person's importance may be revealed in an unassuming or quiet way. Also, someone's significance may not be easily understood. Though we may often think of an illness or a disability as something that gets in the way of life, something negative; maybe it can be positive, even a purpose in life. Darla had other life purposes such as her love of animals, but the way she handled her illness seemed to be a purpose. Her life was very different from most children's. She chose a positive way to deal with her illness and taught us. It was all a learning experience, for her and for us. If everything in life had gone perfectly, with no challenges, would we have grown? When things were not as we planned, we learned to better appreciate our lives, our health, and our world. Darla's views helped us to be grateful and to live our own purposes.

Darla's experience of having cancer was very valuable for many living now. She went through medical treatments that paved the way for better treatments and cures. She tried out a prosthetic leg and that experience led to better prosthetics. Many people with cancer today get well and go on to live long healthy lives. Many can live fuller lives with the wonderful new prosthetics.

LESSONS

I received so many gifts from Darla. She touched my life and shaped me. Here are some insights I received from being with her:

People choose when to pass on

When I cared for my mother at the end of her life, I was upset that I had been with her for a couple of weeks with few breaks and yet I was gone when she passed away. I felt not only guilty but also deprived of being there. Her hospice nurse explained that, though some like to be surrounded by loved ones when they pass, often a person waits until their main caregiver is away. This can make it easier to separate from them and leave this world, as they must. A friend's mother waited for her family to step out of the room before passing alone. I heard Darla waited until her parents had gone out and Dianna was out of the room.

I felt bad that Darla was alone and felt guilty for briefly leaving my mother until I was told it was likely their choice of timing. It helped me a great deal to understand this and not take it personally. I've shared this with others who had a similar situation and they've much appreciated receiving peace from that insight.

Death is not to be feared

In multigenerational homes, children are often present when their grandparents or others pass on. Death is an expected and normal part of life. Many people with terminal illnesses use their time for sharing and connecting deeply. Some are even video recording aspects of their lives during their illnesses. They wish to share with loved ones or give others some understanding of their experiences. Their insights, thoughts, and feelings are valuable. Like Darla, many are more aware of the wonder and goodness of life, often overlooked in our busy lives. Being open to sharing can be healthy. It can heighten gratitude and ease the fear of death.

Darla wasn't anxious, knowing that she would soon pass on. Rather, she was excited because she believed that she would soon be in heaven with God—her biggest adventure! Some believe they will simply cease to exist at death. Others believe we go to heaven or to the other side of a veil. Believing that we will see loved ones again helps many people. It helps me. But all beliefs should be respected. Whether or not people believe in God or life after death—these are personal choices and everyone should be allowed to pass on in peace. Though I share my thoughts and beliefs here, I understand that everyone has different experiences that form their beliefs. It's okay. Some people don't understand why their family member or friend would not continue treatment for a disease, or wish to pass on as soon as possible. These are choices that we can accept, even if we can't understand them. Especially at this time of life, acceptance is a gift.

Hospice programs are very beneficial. Hospice workers talk openly about death and help people prepare in a peaceful, loving way. I was glad to have the time to say goodbye to Darla and my mother, saying all that needed to be said and showing love. On the other hand, the accident that took my father's life allowed no time for that closure. I was glad he didn't suffer an illness, but I wish it hadn't been so abrupt. I believe that only a veil separates us. He is with me, just differently. I tell him I love him now. I believe we are with God and souls are connected, during this life as well as before and after it.

Ask for and give help

Sometimes life gets really hard. How did Darla live with her challenges? Life was difficult and yet she appreciated the good she had, including people to help her. Let nature and animals lift your spirits. Let people in. Let them help you. Interestingly, when we need people the most, we sometimes push them away. Maybe we have to give up pride and ask for help. Maybe we need to ignore embarrassment or gather some courage. We need to realize that sometimes we need to share our negative feelings, to be real. Many hurting people hide behind smiles. Perhaps necessary at times, this deception hinders getting help. Most people will not recognize a false smile. They will accept that all is well. Some people find it hard to reach out, as in depression. Push yourself to find help. Sometimes people reach out and still don't find help. Keep trying.

We can't always fix everything, but when people ask us for help, we should do as much as we can. Give them help or aid them in securing support. Show love and give hope with simple words like "I care"—and listen. Listen. Just be there. It is not always possible to know the best course of action. Sometimes leaving people alone is good and sometimes offering a heart-to-heart conversation is better. Often, we need to get someone to a counselor, maybe multiple counselors to find the right one. Issues like depression are not always recognized, but some things may point to issues such as sleeping too much, not showing emotions, or not caring about favorite activities. We need to beware of judgments. For example, it doesn't help to call someone lazy for oversleeping if it is a symptom of their depression. As you can imagine, judgmental statements could be detrimental, pushing someone further away. A person's thoughts or feelings are real to them. Criticism is not helpful. Something may not make sense to you, but it does to them. We all have differences in thought, too. We may think we are right, but maybe our thoughts aren't right for others. We don't want to hurt someone already in pain. It can be difficult. Our goal is to reduce potential harm.

Interestingly, people will often be patient and feel sorry for someone with an illness like cancer yet not for someone with a mental illness. Why? A mental condition can be just as challenging to people and their families as a physical one, especially if long term. Sometimes, a condition like depression occurs due to a physical issue, presenting a double struggle. An example might be someone who is suddenly in a wheelchair or paralyzed—or in extreme, unceasing pain. Someone worrying about a loved one in such a condition, or a caregiver, can be depressed. The mental stress in the case of a physical illness seems better understood than primary mental conditions. This difficulty in understanding is a reason we need to look more carefully and be more alert to mental and emotional issues.

Some people don't seem to have strong feelings. They don't seem bothered by much. They don't seem happy, either. Perhaps some of these people have very strong feelings that they tamp down because the feelings are too much to handle. Perhaps they feel so much that they lock the feelings away to make themselves more comfortable. They might not even realize it. Many people may need encouragement to share important thoughts and feelings.

If we want to help, a good way to begin is with knowledge. Reading and professional consultations are good for understanding. If we need help, we must ask. Even if doors seem to shut on us, we need to be open to help, to love. There is always goodness to let in. We have power. We may not be able to change what happens to us, but we can choose to be the best we can be, again and again.

Focus on the positive and the present

Too much energy is spent being stuck in the past or worrying about the future. The past is over. Rehashing a troubling part of life, as many of us do, isn't helpful. Stop those negative thoughts from replaying in your head. Suffering, sadness, something you think you've done wrong or you think others have done wrong ... it's over! Forget. Forgive others. Forgive yourself. Forgiving others can set you free. It's good to let go of things that cause pain or harm and focus only on things that are absorbing and emitting positive energy. This can mean letting go of situations, things, or people. There is no need to let yourself be hurt. Often it is best to just do what you can and then wish situations and people well, give them to God, and let go. Move on to the positive. Live! Darla taught me to focus on the positive—in the present. It's not easy, but I try hard to follow her great example. I believe Darla saw her illness as positive, in that it created a chance for spiritual growth. I can now see going through my difficult situations as a spiritual journey, though I can't say I always thought that way while going through them. We don't welcome pain or hardships. Gratitude comes when we realize there can be positive effects and growth.

Darla didn't worry about the past or the future. She was freed from such thoughts. Toward the end of her life, she knew everything she did might be for the very last time. That led her to truly pay attention to everything. She really appreciated all of the good! She loved to hold her precious baby niece, fussy or not. She appreciated any help she was given. She also appreciated laughter. When we could have a real belly laugh or let loose singing, it felt good! She made the most of every single day. How many of us truly pay attention to beauty, love, and joy? Anyone who helps us or treats us kindly is showing love. Do you notice flowers, smiles, a blue sky, the colors of your food, and squirrels? Beauty! Wait, squirrels? To me, the furry little critters with the fluffy tails are beautiful—until they get into my attic. (Forgive me, Darla, they don't get to live in my home.) I'm still working to pay attention to beauty. When I first come home after a vacation in the desert, I notice and admire our beautiful green trees. However, a mere few days later, they seem normal. When I am in the high desert of Sedona, Arizona, I can start ignoring the wondrous red rocks. It's crazy. I have to remind myself to be aware!

Grounding is important—becoming focused, connected, and aware. I try to stay in the present, but it is so tempting to fall back into bad habits and get caught up in worries about the past and future. Focusing on one thing in the present takes practice and lots of restarts for me.

A simple example: I can be chopping vegetables and start thinking of something I need to do in the future or perhaps something I did in the past, maybe something I view as a problem that I feel I need to fix. Now, two things happen. First, I leave the present and worry needlessly because this isn't the time for fixing anything. In fact, any worry is needless. Does worry ever fix or change anything? Maybe it can motivate, but action changes things, not worry itself. Second, I could end up chopping my finger in my wandering state of mind. Even positive thoughts of the past or future can take my thoughts off the chopping. Consider being unfocused while hiking along a cliff or simply crossing a busy street. I imagine many accidents are due to unfocused, wandering minds. Stay present!

How often do we miss part of a conversation because we are thinking of something we just said or what we might say next? Maybe we start thinking of an earlier conversation? I think most of us do this often. I can find myself thinking of an answer before the other person is finished talking. Sadly, I realize I missed half of what was said and have to ask them to repeat it. Listening workshops teach staying present to focus on what's being said. Listening is more than just hearing. Listening is much more active, trying to truly understand another person. It's amazingly hard to listen because many of us think multitasking is a good thing in our fast-paced world. We tend to lose the present. Many moments in life end up totally missed! Listening with care could vastly improve our relationships.

Toward the end of her life, Darla was in an incredible sort of bubble that allowed her to be focused on the present and happier in her condition, which to most of us would seem considerably hard. She didn't have to worry about her future. Her past mattered, of course, but she didn't worry about changing any outcomes from it. She had no expectations of how life should be, no future cares or desires. She could just enjoy the present. Each day, the present was her priority, each moment. She chose to see and appreciate her blessings, big and small. She was astonishingly happy. She was awesome. Being with Darla during her life, especially the end of it, I saw an incredible way to live. Thankfully, I can apply it to my life before going through an illness as she did. It's good to live in the present moment and be happy with what I am and what I have. I treasure my blessings much more deeply when I adopt Darla's focus and positivity. I appreciate what I have right now—food and water, a heated home, and good health. I am grateful to have loving people in my life and faith in God and goodness.

Love can come with the pain of loss, but it is absolutely worth it

Love makes life worth living. It's the most important thing in life. If someone believes in God or believes that loved ones who have passed are with them in spirit, they can have the feeling of a friend anywhere, at any time. If someone believes in a connection of all, each thing in nature can be a friend … animals, trees, rain, anything. We are surrounded by love. Everyone should love themselves as well. That was a new concept to me a decade ago, but I believe it is necessary for serenity—to know that we are inherently important, good, and lovable.

Loving friends and family, including pets, are cherished gifts. Unfortunately, all living beings pass away. We must occasionally go through the difficult time of a loved one's death. Yet, although the loss of this love causes us pain, love is very worth it. Life is so much richer. We prove this each time we lose a loved one and choose to love again.

Just four months after Darla died, my father died. It was sudden, a small plane crash. We waited a full weekend to get news. I couldn't stay in the house waiting. My friend's mother tried to feed me, but food tasted like chalk and my stomach was in knots. I rode and rode my bike. When a civil air patrol chaplain came to our door, I thought he was bringing Dad home. I was elated! But my joy was quickly lost when my mother fainted and I realized my family was crying all around me. No, the chaplain had told us of Dad's death. From joy to grief in seconds. I hadn't heard the chaplain's words, or maybe I didn't want to. Just like when I was told about Darla, my brain didn't accept the news. My thoughts stumbled over one another until my world stopped, again. I finally understood and wept, again. It was too soon after Darla died, I could hardly bear it.

It feels like yesterday that I had to fill out the school forms. I was barely managing my grief so I was not ready to start the new chapter of my life, high school. Not wanting to shout out that my dad just died, I got myself up and shuffled to the front of the class, knowing everyone was staring. I whispered to the teacher, "How do I write my father's name if he just died?" It turned out I wasn't to write his name at all. I wrote, "Deceased." That hurt. It was as if he had never existed. Darla was gone. Dad was gone. And, perhaps from the stress, my mother had a lung disease for about a year. She was extremely tired, working while ill. We were thankful my oldest sister moved home for a year to help out.

My father's death was incredibly heartbreaking for me, especially right after living through more than two years of Darla's illness and death. I had little time to grieve Darla and was certainly not ready to lose my father. He had been my rock and a good friend. Dad and I would talk many evenings while listening to ball games and music on the radio. He listened as I poured out my heart about Darla and he answered my questions about life. Both night owls, we would sit out at night and wait for rain, in Phoenix. Yes, pretty silly. People often say it never rains in Phoenix. It is almost true since it rarely rains. So, when there was even a tiny chance of a storm, we sat out on the front porch. We might see a twirling dust devil or rolling tumbleweeds while we waited to feel the refreshing drops and breathe in the wonderful smell of rain. Most often, we smelled only heavy dust that the wind swept in. That would quickly take us back inside. Even so, we loved to sit out and chat.

When Dad died, it was brutal. The two people I could talk to about anything were both gone within four months. I had just been to Darla's funeral. I did not want to repeat it. I can't remember one thing about Dad's funeral. There is no recollection at all—not one memory from that day. I might have gotten closure from his funeral, but no. I didn't see a peaceful body when Dad died. The casket was closed so I could not see my father after his death. I was simply told he was gone. I saw him in dreams, smiling at me from crowds. As a fourteen-year-old child, the dreams made me wonder if he might still be alive. Maybe it was all a mistake.

Realistically, I knew better, but I didn't understand the dreams. Some say that people who have passed visit their loved ones through dreams. If that's true, I wish I had understood it. Two deaths and my mom being very ill was a lot of loss at once. Ruth, much like another mother to me, couldn't help me because she also had a second death to grieve soon after Darla passed away. My guidance system was gone.

I was devastated and went into a tailspin. I struggled a lot during my high-school freshman year. At school, my eyes were either glazed over or blurred with tears. I didn't care about school or much else. I often sat and stared out from the porch I had shared with Dad, his chair empty. So empty. Just as I had felt after Darla passed—everything looked the same, but nothing was the same. I feared sitting on the porch at night. I realized I hadn't worried about the dark when Dad was with me. There was a chill in the house but not from the cold. Mom was grieving and ill, and her tailbone was injured from fainting at the news. Everyone was in shock. It was amazing how things could change so quickly. Ironically, I thought, *I should talk to Darla.* But, not an option. I chose another option—I went to scary drinking parties on weekends to escape the pain. This caused me to lose many friends, creating more pain. They were jumping whole-heartedly into exciting high-school life and I was stuck in overwhelming grief. I felt like I was trudging through thick mud. Slow motion. The alcohol numbed the pain but poorly. Lessening pain is not healing. We need to work through our pain to be well and I wasn't doing that. I was avoiding it. Many friends distanced themselves from me while my behavior was so different. I couldn't blame them. I do not advise using alcohol when grieving. It is a terrible idea for a teenager, for anyone. My self-esteem plummeted. I had suicidal thoughts. Getting through each day was a major accomplishment. It did gradually improve, but for a whole year, I wasn't on an even keel.

I had other events that were difficult in high school, including a bad leg injury that kept me from my dream of the school pom-pom dance line and other sports. I had to drop out of the dance line just as it started. New methods of coping got me through. At the beginning of my sophomore year, I had come to a time of decision. I could continue sinking or pull myself out and move on. It was a "What would Darla do?" moment. Well, she was a swimmer. She would not sink. I stopped drinking when I met some lovely new girls who introduced me to a religious teen group that straightened me out. I also met a very nice guy in the group who helped me a great deal. The group had a lot of fun times like swimming and playing irrigation football on a large field that was heavily watered on occasion. Great sloppy fun, especially when my face was pushed two inches away from the muck. I was glad they didn't really want to push me in! Teenage antics. We went on inspirational retreats in the woods where we could safely talk about our challenges and get loving support. Those retreats were deep and life-changing. Many were held in the mountains that I loved. I could finally talk about my troubles and let go of much of the pain while having fun. We delivered food to the poor and did other charity projects. I also joined our school's girls' service club. It's much harder to think about your own troubles when helping others. Charitable activities are perfect win-win diversions!

Sometimes I wonder what my life would have been if Darla were still in the world or if my father had lived a much longer life. Wonderful in many ways. I often wished for that life but it was not to be. The growing pains were not pleasant, downright horrid at times, but the experiences helped me grow deeper roots. I am more empathetic and I am stronger. I believe those challenges led me to be more spiritual than I might have been. I'm grateful for my growth.

I remained close to Ruth during my teen years. She even taught me to drive. She was so patient and kind. Another special family also helped me through my ordeal. I am very thankful for all the incredibly caring people who helped me during my teen years. I am especially thankful for having Dad and Darla in my life, even for such a short time. They are everlasting blessings to me. Being unconditionally loved makes life wonderful. Kind and caring people are treasures. I would never give up love, even knowing that close relationships can end for many reasons including death, divorce, breakups, disagreements, and moving. Yes, these situations can be very unpleasant and, to be honest, at times I prayed never to have such hardships again, but what would be the alternative? Not having love at all. No. I would have missed so much and don't want to close off to it. Love is precious. It is the reason for living.

Each time I saw my children make a special close friend, I renewed my openness for love. I watched in awe as their faces lit up when that friend entered the room. They would drop everything and run to that person. I find it completely fascinating that out of a huge number of people, one will catch our attention. Why? Perhaps we can explain being drawn to someone by having similar preferences or appreciating their appearance, but not always. Sometimes there is just a spark for no apparent reason—something about a person that makes you feel excited, content, and whole. People may even feel like magnets, leaning toward one another. This is a connection for life, and maybe beyond. Darla, my friend, your spark was well worth the pain of loss. We will meet again.

Connection

What do people truly need to be happy and healthy? Friendship. Deep friendship is love, though we may not always think of it as the same. Humans need connection. We are social beings. Sometimes we see this very clearly when a person touches us so profoundly that our lives are changed forever, like my life with Darla. Other times, we connect simply—a smile to or from a stranger or by opening a door for someone with their hands full. Often, we don't realize how much we can help someone or how much we need others. It is good to understand it. We start chain reactions in positive or negative ways, even with small actions. Really, we don't have a choice whether or not to affect others. Everything we do spreads out to others—the ripple effect. If we are nasty to someone, they can be mean to another. If we smile, that person may engage positively with the next person they see. Maybe after I gave my radio to my patient to calm her, she was nicer to the nurses than she might have been, and then the nurses were nicer to their patients ... a great chain reaction. We all have challenges and bad days that might cause us to be unpleasant or unhelpful, but, like Darla, we can choose positivity. We can focus on just today and make it good. Then, do it another day, on and on. It's always in our power to smile. We also have the choice to ignore someone or to scowl. Our choice! Scowling isn't likely to make points with anyone, unless they are in the mood to find it funny. Or, one kind act can make someone's day. Last New Year's Eve, I went dancing alone. Some friends were there and I made some new ones. One friend put a flashing ornament in my hair. It was a seemingly small thing, but the caring gesture meant a lot to me! It made me feel included. I was very grateful. One act of kindness a day is a great idea and, in fact, there is an organization called just that. Many people see a warmhearted action and want to copy it. Good!

Often people don't realize that they do something nice for themselves as much as for the other person. The helper's high, a release of the feel-good brain chemicals called endorphins, is a return gift. What a perfect way to get high, from doing good works. Much better than drugs or alcohol. The givers and receivers get to feel great! Parties and other sorts of gatherings can also be a way to bring people together in a positive, joyful way. Organizations can unite people with similar interests. "The more, the merrier" phrase works for many people, yet not everyone is comfortable with groups. Sometimes just two make a great connection, like Darla and me. Darla also had a girls' church group that did good works and had good times. Find a group or person to play or work with, whatever suits you.

In many societies today, people are less connected. We keep ourselves busy, sometimes too busy to pay attention to others. We have many devices that take up our time and energy. Decades ago, I remember hating the thought of our family in separate rooms with different devices. Too much separation for me. We had to insist on family dinners, game nights, and outings—enough times of connection to know each other. People may be geographically separated, too, with many living alone and far from friends and relatives. We need to realize the importance of true connection—listening, caring, and being there for each other, especially in times of need. We can find and enjoy like-minded people, as people tend to do, and still be inclusive and open.

Thinking about strangers connecting, stories of subways come to mind. Many different scenarios can play out in subways. Sometimes people are harassed or even hurt. Other times, a stranger may be tired, sad, or lonely, and a person talks with them to brighten their mood. We hear about people playing an instrument or starting a sing-along in subways. Suddenly strangers start smiling at one another. Moods can change very quickly. Such power in our choice of actions!

It's interesting that when a natural catastrophe strikes, like fire or flooding, people often ignore differences and work together. Suddenly, the same people who were at odds or are total strangers work together toward a common goal. It's nice when a catastrophe is not needed for cooperation.

Though the goal is to feel our connection to all, it is often easier for many to feel connected when they have commonalities. People often help others in the same area when a disaster strikes. Some help people from the same church, or with similar troubles, or similar enjoyments. When we have something in common, we feel a connection. But, maybe we have more commonalities than we believe. Maybe we can look more broadly. One of my favorite books, *The Elegance of the Hedgehog*, has a good lesson. I was reminded that we should not judge a person by what we quickly see. Many aspects are hidden and perhaps what we think we know is incorrect. For example, many shy people are thought to be rude or unfriendly. People with hearing issues can be thought to be rude for not answering a question they never heard. Some people actively hide who they are, trying to be what is expected. A character in the book hides her intelligence and other traits to fit what people expect of her. This might serve a purpose for her, but it mostly keeps people away. As other characters get to truly know her, she makes new friends. If we are open and share, we may find a deep connection when we least expect it.

The times I've shown or talked about my imperfections, physically or emotionally, are the times I've felt more connected to people. Others will join in conversations. Being open and real allows for better communication. People seem to shy away from perfection. Often people feel they shouldn't show true feelings. Almost everyone I know well has some insecurities they don't usually share. When someone admits imperfection, another feels more comfortable and shares more openly. Someone sharing deep feelings or something interesting about themselves seems to work similarly. I can much more easily talk with someone who has shared something deep and genuine.

Lives are stories to share. Open up. Make heartwarming connections.

Let love guide, not fear

Darla could have been fearful but she didn't let that rule her. She didn't fear the future or what others thought of her. She didn't dwell on other people's opinions when she had her life to live! Instead, she loved God and others and went out to live in that love. Fear should not stop us from making the most of each day.

I love that most of the stories about people with differences end with them going out and fully living … the Elephant Man, Wonder, the woman with the facial birthmark, and many real-life stories. It is great that many people are leaving fear behind. They are taking the chance to thrive.

Shyness and fear can stop a life. Darla rescued me during my first huge change, moving away from my friends and a large part of my extended family as a child. She helped me to open up to others. Even now, I often stop myself from doing things due to shyness. I feel awkward in many situations. I haven't completely lost all the fears of the little girl in those hard times and still work at being confident. Darla had a strong spirit of calmness and strength. I call on that serenity to open myself to other people and situations. To become more like her, I do deep breathing and meditation. It allows me to stop sadness or anxiety and experience new things and help where needed—to truly live life. I love to dance, almost any type. It's great exercise and gets me out with people. It has physical and emotional health benefits, and mental benefits when learning a new dance! Sometimes, if there is somewhere I want to go for music and dancing but I can't find a friend to go with, I'll go alone. A few people have mentioned that I'm brave to go alone. It's true, especially because I am shy. However, for me, it's a case of living in love or living in fear. Sometimes fear wins and I stay home, but that happens less and less. Fun and being with people are important and I want to live fully. I want to think with my heart and override fear. I just met a new group of wonderful people by getting involved with collecting coats and blankets for the homeless. I was nervous but did fine, and now some people are warmer! Darla would be proud of me. I nurture myself with nice people and wonderful dancing so I can help when needed.

During my many years of delivering Meals on Wheels, I've met numerous interesting people. I met a lovely blind lady. She needed extra oxygen, so she always had a tank. She was not fearful, being blind and vulnerable. She was quite peaceful. Acceptance of what couldn't be changed created peace for her. She had lived a fascinating life. She was happy and accepting of her limitations in her present time. The only time I saw her flustered in many years was at her nursing home after she could no longer be in her own home. I was visiting and found her out in the hall, very distressed. The electricity had gone out and her oxygen was off. Luckily, someone soon came to help. Even then, she calmed down quickly. So like Darla, she dealt with her issue and moved on to being happy. She was a great role model.

We need to look at our fears and realize the basis of our thoughts. Were we taught to fear? If so, we can change it. A story about snakes comes to my mind when I think about fearing or judging without knowledge. When my daughter was in middle school, the science teacher was looking for a summer home for the school's snakes. I can't imagine why, but parents didn't want snakes in their homes. I was begged to please take them! They were corn snakes about 3 feet long and about as wide as a thumb. They were a beautiful orange color with black and white stripes. Some years earlier, we had gerbils that made me nervous until I grew to love the furry little guys. Again, I was nervous, but I decided I could feed the snakes for just three months. Three months was only six feedings! Well, again, Darla would have been proud. I turned out to be a good snake mom. Every two weeks, I would warm frozen mice in hot water and dangle them at the snakes with forceps. Only the forceps were between their mouths and me. And when they opened their jaws, it was scary how big those mouths were. The snakes would spring up, snatch the mice, and be back down before you could blink. I had to mentally fasten my feet to the floor not to jump when the snakes did. They were lightning fast, giving no warning. The first feeding was terrifying! Then, it became a bit less terrifying but never comfortable. Gradually, we realized the little creatures had very different personalities. The male was quite shy. When he was laid out on my forearm, he would double back to lay his head on my arm. I would even say he cuddled. The female would stretch way out from my forearm to look around, bobbing her head every which way, curious about everything. What was around to play on? When in their aquarium, she was often way up out of the pine shavings to look around whereas you could barely see the male's eyes as he peeked out. They were very nice as long as we paid attention to when they were shedding their skins. That was the only time they got crabby. We just respected them and let them be for a couple of days. After shedding, they were sweet and ready to play again. How do snakes play? They would slide around on us and anything else. My son has curly hair and it was longish with tight curls. The snakes would glide through his curls. We had a double-wide papasan chair with a woven wicker base. We'd take off the cushion and let them weave around the wicker. They seemed to have a great time. Now, I know many people would call me crazy to like snakes. I would have said the same thing before having them. However, the little critters were quite easy to care for and they were very nice and fun! This isn't much different from being afraid of certain people. Once we are able to know the personality of someone we fear, that fear may be gone. Preconceived notions may disappear when we understand people. We may accept and enjoy, or even love, someone we feared.

Compassion and service

Everybody needs help sometimes: physically, mentally, or emotionally. What a great world we could create if we cared about and helped each other without reservation. I love this popular parable. Many people were sitting at a round table. In the middle of this table was a big bowl of hot and delicious stew, but the people were all starving. Their spoons were way too long. They couldn't get the food from the bowl to their mouths. They were miserable and crying. In the next room, the environment was exactly the same. Several people were seated at a round table. A hot, savory bowl of stew sat in the middle. Again, their spoons were much too long. However, these people were not at all miserable. They were well-fed and laughing. Why? They were feeding each other—caring and sharing. A lovely way to live! Help or smile at someone, especially someone having a bad time. It's tempting to ignore someone in a bad mood. However, that is when we most need to help and be kind. It is also important to help when we are needed, not only when we wish to be helpful. There is a difference. It is putting someone else above ourselves sometimes. A great way to make a new friend is to lend a hand. Keep your eyes open to see opportunities. Some people are ill at ease in asking for help. This can be the case for people with disabilities. Some are very independent but some may need help physically or fitting in to a crowd. In fact, someone doesn't have to have a disability to need help fitting into a crowd. People who are open and inviting are very needed. Being alert for opportunities to guide and help is important. In the parable above, just one person needed to look into the eyes of another across the table and want to feed them. I can easily see this happening with one pair and then the others, watching with tilted heads, say, "What a great idea. Let's do it!" Suddenly, there is a roomful of happy people!

There are sayings about making your life count. Some take this to mean doing something really important that will make people remember you. Well, it's great when people do something so large that they live on in history books. However, one of those remarkable and well-known people, Mother Teresa (now Saint Teresa), encouraged helping one person at a time, in uncomplicated ways. I see her advice as both simple and profound. She spoke of a way for everyone to make their lives count. We don't have to do something huge to be special and valuable. We are all valuable, in giving help and in receiving help. Contrary to what we often think, we must do both.

Some people find it much easier to give than to receive. A true giver can be uncomfortable receiving help, a gift, or a compliment. However, it is beneficial, and even necessary, to have the ability to receive as well as give. In the parable above, what would happen if the givers wouldn't receive the food? They would starve. A person can be starving emotionally as well as physically. Caregivers need to be fed, emotionally and sometimes literally, so they don't experience burnout or get sick. They need to accept help. They need to take time for themselves. Givers, or helpers, must be nurtured and have their own needs met in order to continue serving in love. Otherwise, they may be open to illness, resentment, or burnout.

Another point about Mother Teresa is that she seemed to have a wonderfully positive attitude. It is widely written that she suffered from depression and sometimes felt separated from God. Perhaps this is why she had so much compassion for the suffering. When she helped others, she felt better and hopeful. In her work, she focused very much on each person, so she could help without personal or situational sadness paralyzing her. It can be easy to get bogged down when looking at huge problems like hunger and poverty. For example, I'm very grateful for having ample food. However, if I start thinking about those who don't have enough food, I get sad, almost losing my gratitude within negative thoughts. I can feel like giving up because I know I can give to food banks and deliver meals, but I can't feed everyone who is hungry. If Mother Teresa helped one sick person and then despaired that there were too many, she might have given up. She might have given up her purpose of caring for people if the overall severity of the problem overwhelmed her. She didn't let it. She gave out great smiles and cared for people, one at a time. She recruited other helpers, one at a time. It was enough. Look at the chain reaction! How many people are now caring for others, and how many have been helped, because of her? She gave love to each person she helped. She was an amazing person.

When I laughed with Darla, did I cure her cancer? Could I laugh with all the people with cancer? No. I could only smile and put happiness into Darla's life, and into mine. It was enough. It was good. When we smile at someone on the street, maybe a disfigured person, we add happiness to the world. We help a person and add happiness chemicals to our own brains. Nice! We can also give out happiness just by showing our joy.

I believe that helping people is my main purpose in life and my time with Darla greatly enhanced it. It made me feel good to help her when I could. During that rare time that she acted mean and sent me away, in addition to losing her friendship briefly, I lost the ability to give to her. It felt bad. I wanted to help and I was happier when I could. Watching my friend struggle with an illness and disability led me to be more compassionate and understanding. My own experiences of having pain and being different added to my understanding. I am now braver in approaching others with differences. I can accept them and help them when needed. My first volunteer service on my own was at age twenty, driving a Red Cross van to take people with disabilities to plays and parks. I doubt that would have caught my eye without having a one-legged person in my life. Since then I have volunteered often. My paid work has always been in service positions. I loved working in hospitals. I give and also receive good feelings from helping.

That said, I am finally realizing how much I need to improve my receiving skills. These skills are necessary so I don't become angry or resentful, feeling used or overdone. A giver's needs must be met. My eyes were further opened when talking with a friend who had trouble asking for something she needed, or perhaps it was saying no to something she didn't want to do. She said, "I just can't do it. I can't speak up or put myself first." To her, others seemed more important. I totally understood her and suggested, "Maybe you could think that you are not more important but, rather, you are equally important. Your needs are also worthy of attention." She paused to think, answering, "Yes, that I can understand. I can accept that I am equally important." I'm learning to speak up for myself and strike a balance between nurturing myself and others. If my needs are met, I can serve nicely, before feeling upset and possibly speaking improperly. When I don't get nurturing or nurture myself, I can feel that others take advantage of me. Then anger or sadness comes out. Actually, sadness and being hurt can come out as anger, just as fear can come out as anger. When someone's needs are fulfilled, there is good energy available for helping. Service can then be done in love, as it should be. Givers can easily get into a bind in which many expect help and they accuse the giver of being selfish if they don't constantly give.

It's not selfish to consider your own needs. It is simply loving and caring for yourself, who is equally important!

There is a great analogy for this concept. On a plane flight, you are told to put on your oxygen mask before trying to put on someone else's, such as a child. Otherwise, neither person may get oxygen and both may perish. If a caregiver doesn't get what they need, they may not be able to help as well and, eventually, maybe not at all. I was so pleased that Darla's mother had help and people caring for her during Darla's illness. She took on so much. She needed nurturing to replenish her body and spirit.

Thinking about service, it's nice to get something in return when not expecting it. I chuckle as I remember the time I sewed two or three dresses for my sister's wedding. They were yellow, not my favorite color. I didn't want to sew again for a long time, much less immediately for myself. My aunts came to town and asked me what I was wearing to the rehearsal dinner. Not caring much about clothes, I shrugged, "I don't know. I've been too busy sewing to think about it." They didn't like that at all. The dinner was the next day and I was expected to look presentable. Suddenly, all four aunts and my mother swooped in and found some leftover fabric. They were like a giant whirlwind circling around me. They quickly and magically created a pretty skirt and top for me. I felt very happy with their care and attention. I was renewed for helping again.

Understanding can lead to acceptance

I was once on a plane with a very nice boy who had Tourette syndrome. My middle seat was next to his window seat. When I sat down, he waited for me to settle in and then politely got my attention. He wanted to explain to me immediately that he had a difference that might make me uncomfortable. He explained that his Tourette syndrome caused some odd mannerisms. He might say something too loudly, say a bad word, or make a weird noise. It might even seem as if he cursed at me. These noises were not intentional. He couldn't control himself. It was just a part of his condition. He couldn't control his actions, but I could control my reactions. I decided to be tolerant. He did make odd noises, but I remember having a nice long talk with him and enjoying the flight. It was great that he was so open and helped me to understand. By telling me, he made me feel compassionate instead of irritable or angry. I found some noises humorous, though I didn't laugh since he might have been hurt. I was ready to stand up for him if a negative comment was made. I realized later that, without the ability to explain and with a person quick to anger, he might sometime be in danger. It made me sad to envision a time when someone might hurt such a nice boy, physically or otherwise. I hope he always gets a chance to explain or, if not, people are tolerant.

Since I met this boy, I've watched videos of people with Tourette. Sometimes Tourette causes tics like the boy's vocal sounds and mild movements. However, sometimes people have quite severe uncontrolled tics like punching and kicking. They can hurt other people including family, caregivers, and friends. Scary. It's so much more difficult when others don't understand. It is difficult for families since they have to cope as well as watch their loved one go through this tough condition. It is helpful that some celebrities and others are open about having this and similar conditions. A movie was recently made about one man's journey with Tourette, *Front of the Class*. It is the story of Brad Cohen who wanted to be a teacher so much that he kept applying after being turned down many times. Apparently, some people just couldn't imagine how he could teach well with his mild tics and passed him up. Finally, he was hired and became a wonderful teacher like my fifth-grade teacher. He connects incredibly well with his students who understand the syndrome and don't appear at all bothered by his actions. He is now an assistant principal and a great role model. Like Darla and me, he loves chocolate-chip cookies! I wonder if his kids have to hide them like mine did if they wanted any left.

Tourette symptoms are much more tolerable when they are understood, often to the point of being ignored. I hope the story of Brad's success improves acceptance of this difference. His success gives us all encouragement not to give up on our dreams.

People with mental disorders may have an additional challenge. Mental disorders like depression and anxiety can still have a stigma, a negative attitude, connected to them. In addition, mental differences aren't always seen outwardly, so they are less understood. These people may be bullied and socially isolated. Many people feel that we need to better understand and treat many mental and emotional disorders. People suffering from these types of conditions deserve support and acceptance, just like those with physical differences.

Understanding is trickier when a person has a difference that doesn't show or only shows up sporadically, like Tourette, breathing problems, arthritis, autism, deafness, fibromyalgia, anxiety, or migraines. Some disorders can be extremely painful. Some are constant. I can't imagine having to get through a day with something like severe fibromyalgia, but a lot of people do it. I especially can't imagine coping with something difficult while dealing with angry or intolerant people. It's a small issue, but I've always had problems with one ear because I was born with tiny ear canals, one badly angled. I don't hear well in certain circumstances. My mother sometimes chastised me, saying, "Why don't you listen?" I usually let it go but one time I felt I needed to try again, replying, "I try. You know I often only hear with one ear." This was met with surprise. She knew that but apparently kept forgetting. This time she really listened and I was glad. She finally understood. Good communication. People may act differently due to disorders poorly understood or invisible. Sometimes others just don't know the situation. Misunderstandings can be solved with communication. One time, I watched a lady being angrily questioned when she parked her car in an accessible parking space. The other person was unpleasant and critical until hearing that she had a breathing problem. He assumed someone must have difficulty walking or some other visible disability. We can judge too quickly. It's human. We can forgive judgment that is not malicious. However, it should be checked. It is good for people to be open about their issues so others can better accept and help them. But we also just need to realize that many conditions are unseen and stop judging. People have invisible physical and mental illnesses. They also hide emotional issues such as grieving a recent death, broken heart, or broken dream. Perhaps they just lost a job. Sometimes I wish everyone could just wear signs saying, "My challenge is ...." Then we wouldn't have to wonder. It would be interesting to see how many read, "No issues today!" Wouldn't signs make it easy to know how to approach everyone? We just need to understand that everyone has things to get through, long or short term. Communication is valuable. Patience and kindness go a long way.

After seeing the movie, *Wonder,* I read about strong, spirited people with Treacher Collins syndrome and similar conditions. Some of these children have gone through many, many surgeries. Looking beyond their abnormalities, we can also think about the symptoms caused by the physical differences. A person with a deformed face could have trouble breathing, smelling, seeing, or eating. Pressure on the brain can be painful. Like Darla, they may have gone through a lot and they just want to get out and live normally, doing all the typical things. They deserve it.

Unfortunately, parents of children with differences have stories about the hardships they face. Their children might be ignored or mocked. Since other children might be upset or scared by seeing disfigurements, parents may be shamed for letting their kids be seen out in public. Some people still think disfigured people should be kept at home as they might have been many decades ago. Some still object to seeing deformities. They are not understanding. Perfection is not reality. Children need to know this. Some people are born with differences and many people have something happen to make them a bit different, like Darla's illness requiring her leg to be amputated. This is a fact of life. Kids can be taught to understand and accept everyone. Sadly, some parents are unsure whether to take out their kids with differences due to people's negative reactions. Parenting can be difficult. Ultimately, we want to help our children and we want them to be happy. I hope they all find peace, both sides.

Negative attitudes are sad and very hard on entire families. People with children who have differences often say they would like other parents to teach their children respect, patience, and kindness. We can teach them that people with differences are normal and not to be feared. Let kids talk to people with disabilities when it is an appropriate time. In addition, teach them to think before acting. That is good advice for any age. By thinking before acting, we will likely make better decisions. Good decisions are important when speaking. We need to take care with words. We've likely all said things we wish we could take back. It all comes down to respect, taking care to show respect. We can feel sad for people, but we should understand that they just want to fit in and feel included. They want to be treated normally, not pitied. Stares and leaving them alone may not as bad as mocking but can be hurtful. People with differences are normal people with normal emotions. They are happy, sad, shy, lively, calm, nervous, embarrassed, excited, etc. They just happen to look or act a bit differently. It's okay. Kids with differences just want to be themselves. Let's let them.

Stand up for others, nicely

Standing up for Darla or for people like the boy with Tourette became a goal for me. Saying something positive to change the situation is always best. "So and so is nice," will often do, though sometimes an explanation is needed. I was very proud of my kids when they came home from grade school and told me about supporting a friend. They just went up and stood with the child being teased so he would feel better and not be alone. Luckily, confrontation was unnecessary. People just being there with him had diffused the situation. The point was made that he had buddies who didn't like teasing or bullying. It can be hard to put yourself out there, but we would all like a champion or two to help us in bad situations. Talking with the person being hurt and making positive plans is very helpful. Bullies may need help as well. We might want to accept a person, but not poor behavior. The differentiation can be difficult sometimes, but it's important to remember. Good people can do bad things in some situations. Perhaps people aren't aware of the harm they cause. Some may act badly because they need help. It's all about respecting other people.

A word of caution because this area can be tricky: safety is a key consideration. Authorities and trained people are often necessary for dealing with some issues. I am advocating simply backing a friend or schoolmate, saying, "Hey, Johnny is doing his best." or "Johnny may look different but he is very nice." It's always better to talk with kids to stop poor behavior at a young age, when they first begin to notice differences.

Someone with a mental or physical disorder may have a behavioral issue. We need to be tolerant, but we need to address unacceptable behavior. Help them get what they need to control a symptom like hitting someone. We obviously can't let people do anything they want. There would be chaos. As on the roadways, there must be order and rules or nobody would get anywhere. Some people need a lot of guidance. Poor behavior that is unintentional, like Tourette cursing and spasms that might create touching someone else briefly, should be tolerated whenever possible. For more serious symptoms, the person should be helped and cared for. Communicating something like severe Tourette syndrome is helpful to increase understanding. Anyone who understands can then stand up for them if needed. Communication is a great way to help yourself, like the boy on the plane. People working together to find a solution is ideal. Create peace.

Anyone could
quickly be different

We should act according to the golden rule: treat others as you would like to be treated. Josh Blue, a comedian, said, "Whenever people are being mean about disability, I think they don't realize that not only are we the largest minority group on the planet but we're also the only minority group that you can join at any time. You're just one bad bike ride away." True. Accidents or illnesses can quickly change us. Some are born with a difference, but any of us could have a difference tomorrow. We might be in a wheelchair or look different with an eye patch, cast, brace, or missing limb. We may be hunched over or limping. Changes can happen in an instant. We would all want to be treated well.

Sometimes someone can be disabled short term. It can give them some understanding of long-term disabilities. Very short term, I know how it felt to look strange to others. I had a bike accident in high school. I had a huge scab on my face, more big scabs down one side of my body, and half of a front tooth missing. Pretty ugly. I was teased by the kids who knew me. Outside of school, people stared and even scooted away from me, maybe thinking it was contagious. I was embarrassed but, after being with Darla, I went out anyway. Later in high school, I had chicken pox and had to go to school with multiple pox scabs. Yuck. Still another time in high school, I hurt my leg and limped for months. Sometimes the muscle would badly cramp and I couldn't walk, curled up in pain. More stares. That's life, I thought. This is my life. If Darla could go out without a leg, I can go out with scabs, limping, or sitting in a heap. People will understand, or not. It's okay.

Some years ago, I had corrective bunion surgery on both feet. When they asked what color I wanted for casts, I said I liked blue. Well, that was a mistake. I had never had a cast and didn't realize I would have these large casts on my feet for months! They didn't show me the blue color either. So instead of a wiser choice, like tan to match my skin, I got big, bright, blue casts. Gigantic, neon-blue feet! After weeks of healing, I was glad to be able to get around and resume helping in my kids' school. I went clunking down the hall like a robot, my body moving side to side. The kids knew me, but I had changed. All down the hall, groups of children actually split in two, hugging the walls to get away from me. Their eyes were wide with fright. I felt badly, for them and for me. Luckily, I only had to feel this for a little while. Imagine the people who live every day knowing they might be feared, taunted, or shunned. No matter how we look, we would all like to be treated nicely and normally. I was lucky. It didn't take but a day or two for the kids to get accustomed to me. They quickly adapted to the lady robot with big, blue feet. Not so scary.

Some accidents have ongoing, long-term effects. I know of a person who was paralyzed and another who lost an arm. One of my best friends had a devastating car accident. One minute she was a vibrant teenager and the next she couldn't walk or care for herself. It was a long struggle but she has an amazing spirit and attitude. After being told she would never walk or have children, she went on to have kids as well as walk down the Grand Canyon! She has been through many surgeries and ongoing pain. She has sported various casts and braces. Through it all, she has been happy and active. Luckily, outwardly, she has only a limp and an atrophied leg. She never let that or the pain stop her. She and her husband helped me a great deal during the first few days after a bad accident. They are both naturally caring people yet I believe all that she has gone through has made them even more understanding and empathetic.

Not all changes are visible. I've never had the best memory. I've hit my head a few times. I was told I was in a car accident as a toddler and bumped hard enough to get a bloody nose. Long ago, I was walking out of a mall and slipped on a spilled drink on the ramp. I had my baby in my arms and had to make a quick decision whether to stop my fall and possibly lose hold of my daughter or grasp her tighter to protect her. I chose the latter and am forever glad. However, my back and head weren't so happy. My tensed body clunked on the pavement and I woke up a while later to many people standing around me. I had lots of pain for days but didn't check my head. Then, when skiing recently, I fell hard on an icy slope, knocking my head and wrenching my neck. That time, I did get a head CT scan to check for bleeding but they can't check for memory damage. Luckily, I don't have major problems but I do have some memory issues that might be due to accidents, not remembering people or coming up with words easily. I just use lots of notepads and let people remind me. I have always had poor depth perception. During my driver's education class, they were unsure whether I should have a license. Thankfully, I got one, and in forty-five years have never had a car accident.

After the skiing accident, I had an eye test for tracking issues. Apparently, my eyes will dart back and forth involuntarily. I don't know what happened or when. So, between depth perception and eye issues, my balance isn't the best, perhaps causing the recent falls. The point is that many of us have accidents that cause damage and some are born with damage that cause something that seems odd or wrong to others. We need to be tolerant when people aren't perfect, physically or mentally. We only see the surface of others. We often don't even understand ourselves.

We never know when things might happen to us, creating differences that make us need help and understanding. For decades, I was accident-free. Then, four years ago, I had two accidents within months. One was the severe skiing injury. It was completely shocking. One second

I was fine and then, boom, I could barely move. I had a concussion, a broken collarbone, and a misaligned spine. It was very scary. I was knocked out and woke up talking to the ski patrollers with no recollection of how I got down the slope and no knowledge of what I had been saying. For an hour, I couldn't remember where I lived. I was living alone so, for the first few days, my friends took me into their home. When I was out of shock and able to move a bit, I left, very grateful for their love and care. During the first week, my back and neck became very tight and the muscle spasms were incredibly painful. This lasted a couple of months. I slept in a recliner because I couldn't easily get in and out of bed. I stayed in my robe for days because clothes were too difficult. Slowly, I adapted. I used pull-on pants and snap shirts. They were very difficult to put on but at least doable, compared to zippers and buttons. I wished I had known about the Velcro clothing. I wore a shawl because getting a coat on was impossible. Simple, everyday activities were hard. To get an idea of just how hard it is to manage normal things with physical challenges, bind your dominant arm and shoulder so you can't use them. Now try to do everything with the other hand—squeeze bottles, make a meal, shower or bathe, wipe, brush your teeth, get dressed, etc. Everything is really awkward and takes twice as long, often much longer. Imagine all of this with terrible pain and the draining fatigue of movement.

By the way, I surely didn't try to attempt mascara. Trust me, I would have looked like a clown and would likely have hurt my eye. During that time, I was very grateful for my wonderful cousin and children who traveled to help me get to the doctor and get frozen foods. After many weeks, I was finally better able to get food and supplies. Getting the seat belt on was the hardest part of driving. I was unable to walk upright for quite a while. I was hunchbacked, couldn't easily move my neck, and used an arm sling. Many people looked strangely at me. I would just smile. I leaned on carts and if I couldn't reach or lift something, I asked for help. I was fairly independent by then but there was no reason not to ask for help when I needed it. Most people were happy to assist. Only a few avoided me. Wow, I had a new understanding of people living with disabilities or pain. I saw the world through the eyes of people with disabilities and now make a double effort to ask if they need help. Sometimes help is simply giving someone extra time and patience to complete something that takes them longer than most people. It's nice when we can recognize growth during difficult periods. It is not all negative. I was slowed down from routine and busyness and challenged to fully view my life. Was I on the right path?

Just a couple of months after I was finally better, I had another fall. I was in a large black hand and wrist brace. I couldn't believe it! This time there was no obvious reason for the fall except my balance was off. Of course, some people asked me if I was uncomfortable with people looking at my brace. Yes, a bit. But again, if Darla could go out with one leg and I could go out as a hunchback, was a brace going to stop me? I heard a couple of comments about being klutzy or accident-prone, having two accidents together. Perhaps this was true but it was hurtful. I was also avoided for further hiking. Later, I found out I had Lyme disease, which also might have affected my balance during the time of the accidents. This may have been an instance of an unseen disease and its effects. Lyme disease organisms can attack many systems in the body including the balance and gastrointestinal systems. Sufferers may have multiple issues and be miserable but it doesn't show. We need to be sensitive to people with unseen problems. Watch for signs of discomfort, such as wincing, holding the body oddly, or lack of attention while their focus is on pain. While I was working in hospitals, I noticed that my severely arthritic patients were often the hardest to please. They were trying to be nice but some were downright grumpy. Often their arthritis didn't show, so they didn't get the sympathy or help they deserved. I realize now that having a whole body hurting is a very good reason for grumpiness. We can't always help people physically but we can be compassionate and sometimes make their lives happier. We learn from having hard times. Hard times can create in us compassion, empathy, and strength.

Darla found strength. She had physical help but needed inner strength to cope with her illness. I found the strength to find ways to get better and stay positive. Often people need help when they are suddenly hurt. An injured person may not be thinking correctly. A normally docile dog can bite when it is in severe pain. A person may be irritable or be dazed and disconcerted, not finding their way. Anyone who is hurting can use an advocate, for emotional and mental support as well as physical help. This is true if someone has challenges for a short or long time. It can be difficult to find support in our independent society. Churches, Meals on Wheels, and home health agencies can help, if not friends or relatives. However, one needs help just setting that up. Shock and limitations can make it hard to think well enough to realize what is needed. I did Meals on Wheels for eighteen years and I couldn't think to call them when I needed meals. Help in setting up aid can be done from miles away via the phone or internet, but we first have to understand the need for support.

See the person inside

What is truly important? From being with Darla during her illness, especially in the hospital after her amputation, I learned to look at people for who they truly are, not focusing on their appearances.

A friend who liked to discuss people with me was appalled that I couldn't remember someone's hair or eye color, if they had long hair or facial hair, whether or not they wore glasses, what clothing they wore, etc. I couldn't explain why I didn't notice. I was once embarrassed when my friend said she had on long hair extensions. I also didn't notice that another friend let her hair go gray. I wondered about myself. Was I truly odd? Maybe. Maybe my memory was to blame? That may be partially true, but I realized that I do look into people's eyes. I just do it differently. I don't really care about eye color so I see people's moods and possible needs instead. I notice when people are sad or upset. I don't really care about clothes. Now I view this irregularity as a blessing, though I can still be embarrassed by it. I think it's good to see people in their entirety, not just their bodies. When I saw Darla in the hospital as her true self, I forgot all about her missing leg. She was simply my wonderful friend. I could act normally with her again. Outside stuff matters very little. A physical difference doesn't change a person inside. We need to look beyond the outside appearance.

In fact, facial expressions can be hiding true natures. People can misunderstand expressions. For example, I can look angry when I am pensive, trying to figure something out or watching something with interest. People have asked me what's wrong. I was surprised and glad they asked because I hadn't meant to give an impression of anger. It's hard to stop myself but I try to keep myself from forming a frown, now that I know it happens. My own quirk makes me realize that the way I perceive people's moods may be flawed. I can't know the mind of another person and I should never imagine I can know all of someone even if they reveal part of themselves to me. People are way too complex. In addition, some people work hard to hide negative feelings or problems. It really comes down to communication. If I believe I see something, I ask if what I think is actually correct. Can I assist or support them? Respecting wishes to let them be alone is as important as helping. Everyone has their own degree of openness, too. Some people are open books and some prefer to keep their feelings hidden.

It's good to realize that expressions can be hiding true natures and we can jump to conclusions. I remember a Meals on Wheels client well. I first saw only her frown when I delivered her meals. She wore her frown like a hairstyle. For a while, I saw it and made assumptions and judgments. I avoided her as much as I could. Then, I realized why she always frowned. She was stuck in her home alone and didn't even have a well-working TV. It became clear—she was bored and frustrated at not being able to do anything. I bought her an inexpensive television and started bringing my dog to visit her after doing my route, once or twice a week. Just those few changes and she was like a different person. She was really quite charming and loved petting the long, silky fur of my beautiful Shetland Sheepdog. Her face totally transformed. I thought, *I changed a life because of an uplifting little girl with cancer*. This lady might have gone on to show others that they could change—a domino effect of positivity from life with Darla.

I do think it is good not to focus so much on physical attributes. The person inside, the essence of a person, is much more worthy of attention. We hear about people feeling bad about their looks and having procedures not to correct disfigurement, but to fit an ideal. I understand wanting to look your best. However, people should not be criticized into having surgeries. Shouldn't "pretty" personalities be more admired?

APPRECIATE EVERY PERSON

Every person is important. I like these visualizations: millions of drops of water make the ocean and single grains of sand create a beach. Isn't it the same with people? Nobody is inconsequential. We all make up humanity. We are all here together. It only makes sense to treat each other well. If everyone saw the goodness in others and sought to value and help them, we would have a truly wonderful world.

We all have the light of God within us. Every baby born is perfect in its own way, in God's eyes—whether they are disabled, disfigured, or physically "correct." Some people have a perfect baby, with a difference. People often don't know what to say when a baby is born with a difference, like spina bifida or a missing limb. Some people are so nervous and unsure of what to say that they don't say anything, as when Darla lost her leg. People can just disappear. How sad. If a child is born with a difference or not, congratulations are in order! All babies are lovable little beings. Look beyond a physical issue and welcome a new little one. Offering help and support would be wonderful, but show happiness as well as concern for them. Being there for a parent in this situation is important. They are going through many emotions. Sometimes it takes time and patience to work through the emotions and get back on an even keel. It's hard enough to have a newborn, especially as a first-time parent. With medical challenges, more care may well be needed, for the parents and the child.

I had a baby who couldn't eat for his first five days. We were terribly frightened for him and I called everyone I could think to call. Our fear was understandable since, halfway through the pregnancy, it was found that our first baby had passed away earlier. In addition, our first nephew lived only nine days. It was terrifying. Finally, with the aid of a wonderful La Leche League woman, we figured out that his tongue was sticking to the roof of his mouth so he couldn't suck. I had to hold his tongue down for him and teach him to keep it down. Unfortunately, I believe his digestive system was altered. He cried often for about three months and didn't sleep much. People would look at him and say, "My, he's very thin!" and look at us with pity or with an expression that said, "Feed the poor child!" Most people didn't want to hear why he was so thin. They just unfairly judged. Luckily, our son grew out of this and then slept and ate a lot to make up for the first three months. He quickly gained weight. Just a couple of months later, we were hearing that he was too fat and that we should watch what he ate. Argh! It was hard to stay quiet.

People can be quick to judge parents. We were doing our best with little sleep and little knowledge. He was finally getting healthy and we were thrilled. We didn't need judgments about his care. Comments and advice can be disheartening unless someone knows and can help the situation. This is true in any situation. Imagine if Darla's mother was questioned about care. I was extremely grateful for the woman who finally got food into our son. My mother cared for him some evenings and his other grandparents came to visit so we could get some sleep during those first few months. Kind words and real help were much appreciated! Without the help, I might have been too tired and missed one of my most precious memories—my son seeing his hands and realizing he could move them at will. He was mesmerized by this and I was mesmerized by him.

I often think of new parents and wish them well, especially parents who have a child with health challenges. Give the little ones and their parents extra love. Welcome to all those precious newborns.

Think ahead to these sweet little babies becoming toddlers who haven't yet learned to judge, as well as toddlers who have a difference but haven't realized they are different. Very young children will grab anyone's hand and start playing. Pure acceptance. They simply see a human, or any living being since they're also open to animals and bugs, and enjoy them. Everyone and everything is a friend. It's great. Until they realize that someone is different, they don't care. At some point, they will become aware of differences, but they will likely treat people according to what they are told. Imagine a child growing up. There are a few kids who have differences. At first, it seems perfectly normal. Eventually, the child realizes that there are differences. If told that is fine, it's very likely fine. "Suzy has only one leg so she adapts by hopping or wearing her prosthetic leg." "Oh, okay!" "Johnny shouts out words that might not make sense. He doesn't mean to." "Okay!" and off they go. Kids adapt and accept differences. Oh, if we could all stay this way.

Courage to show differences and what can be accomplished

I am very impressed by the wonderful people who talk about and show us their differences. When they open up and share their lives, they improve our understanding of their conditions. We recognize that adjustments may be needed for functionality. We can see beyond physical changes or behavioral differences. The courage of one sharing person may help another be comfortable with their difference and help other people to be accepting. Some of these people wouldn't even call themselves brave. They are simply living their lives. Why would we consider it out of the ordinary that a person with a disability would be out doing whatever they want? Unfortunately, we don't always expect it. I believe that the more people reveal their differences, the more others will confidently step out. More can live as they wish. Many people are inspiring us to be happy just as we are. People don't have to be perfect! Our happiness comes from within us, not from others validating us. We share the richness and wonder of being human. Differences enhance this intriguing life.

Watch the Special Olympics games for people with intellectual disabilities. The athletes are great examples of people living freely. They are using their athletic skills in competition and also having fun. They show their joy of sports during the training and competitions. Many enjoy being on a team (which I think is the best thing about sports). Their spirits shine brightly.

While writing about Darla, I became aware of many news and media stories about beautiful, inspirational people who have not let a difference stop them. They've been able to go beyond these differences that could be limitations. They are encouraging many others, with or without differences, to make the most of their lives. Sometimes their successes include being famous and sometimes it is the simple success of enjoying life. Some of the many examples of inspirational people in the news and media are one-armed surfers, an aerial acrobat who is a little person, and a pilot with quadriplegia. In addition, there are models with Down syndrome, skin disorders, and colostomy bags in view. Many say they are proud to be among the first people to show differences in this way. It's great that they are so comfortable that they can help us expand our awareness and understanding.

They are stepping out and making their mark on the world. We learn from them that, although we may see someone as different from us in a particular way, they are the same in the important ways. And maybe there really isn't a "norm" after all. We all have something we think looks odd or we may feel different sometimes. We all have quirks. We all have limitations. However, some people do stand out in a crowd in an obvious way and some of them are helping us to become more and more open with any differences.

We are also inspired by people who talk about dealing with their depression, anxiety, post-traumatic stress disorder, obsessive-compulsive disorder, or other sometimes hidden issues. They share their differences by telling their stories, including their feelings. They share what they would like people to know and how they would like others to act with them. This insight is extremely valuable.

A difference can make a wonderful talent even more interesting. *My Left Foot* is a movie that depicts a man with cerebral palsy who was a gifted painter and author. He painted with his foot. It seems odd at first but not when you get used to the idea. Why not? An elephant in Thailand can paint with her trunk.

Josh Blue is a hilarious comedian with cerebral palsy who has worked in the field for nearly twenty years. His disability doesn't hinder his talent at all. In fact, he uses it in his acts. One of his jokes is, as he looks at his shaky arm, he needs forty-five minutes to sign an autograph. He's funny and clever!

Josh Sundquist is amazing. Like Darla, he lost a leg to cancer at a young age. He is now an author, speaker, comedian, Paralympic athlete, influencer, and producer and writer for a TV series based on his life. My favorite of his skills is creating incredible Halloween costumes that are perfect for his one-legged body. I love it. He made a great flamingo, balanced on his crutches, his one foot up as a beak. Among other creations, he has also been a goalpost, a Christmas tree, and a gingerbread man with one leg eaten. The gingerbread man was highlighted on the TV show. So creative!

Alvin Law is an incredible person with a great smile. He was born without arms and adopted by wonderful people who helped him become accomplished in more ways than many of us who are "normal." His mother did not accept that Alvin would be in a school for the handicapped. She believed he could adapt to his condition and he did just that. He learned to use his feet to function like hands. He eats, drives, and plays Frisbee with his dog—with his feet! He is extremely talented. He plays the drums, keyboard, and trombone! He educates as he tells his life story on the internet and at seminars, sharing both his challenges and achievements. His presentations are incredibly inspiring and funny. He's a perfect example of someone who has gone beyond his difference and never let it stop him from living life to the fullest. His positive attitude is contagious. He makes me feel like I can do anything I put my mind to. I enjoy watching him play the drums, mostly because of the way he plays, with his feet. How fun! It is great to see anyone enjoying life, but even more so when someone overcomes a challenge to be all they can be. Alvin inspires all who meet him to do the same. We all have fears. We can all pull away from things that seem too difficult or scary. We can learn from Alvin and others to work through it, to strive for excellence and happiness.

I recently enjoyed seeing an autistic man playing with his band, *Blue Spectrum*. Wow. A great band and nice people. Zayne is a wonder on his guitar, with incredible speed and spirit. He plays with the guitar over his head as well as one-handed. He loves playing! The band's website speaks of potential and promise. So fitting. Zayne's parents were told he likely wouldn't be able to do or feel much. Thankfully, that was not to be. Their child went on to teach himself to play the guitar spectacularly. Such a joyful outcome—a triumph! Zayne very much embodies the wonderful message on the band's website that was created by his father, Gene—"Life Is Not To Be Viewed Through The Single Lens Of A Diagnosis But To Be Lived Through The Spectrum Of Potential, Promise And Purpose."

Another band also demonstrates this great purpose. I had the pleasure of seeing some shows featuring two close childhood friends who are very talented and soulful musicians. Their parents nurtured the duo's natural talent. *InnerVision* is the band's clever name. The two friends happen to be blind, but you wouldn't notice. They are great at so many types of music! Sometimes other musicians join their fun. I especially like that they play at nursing homes in addition to many other venues. Genene plays the keyboard joyfully. Sam plays the trombone, guitar, bongos, and harmonica. They both sing beautifully. They have won many competitions! Genene rocks out with Zayne's *Blue Spectrum* and Sam plays with other musicians as well. We are blessed to have them share their music with us.

In reading *Healthy Happy News* (Love that website), I came across a lovely couple sharing their story. They are like any other couple except that they need to make some adjustments. Winston Clements, who has brittle bone disease, has had over 200 fractures in 34 years, 150 by age 12. Despite his pain and physical limitations, his motto is "Your limitations are an illusion." His fractures could have led him to close off from life but, instead, he uses his difference to let him soar into his mission of inspiring everyone to reach their own potential and to strive for acceptance of all. Disabled? No—capable, able. Like Darla, his great faith in God has given him a positive attitude to follow his dreams. He is a wonderful motivational speaker. His lovely wife, Mayfair, joins him on his quest to show that his disorder does not limit him. By revealing their loving relationship, they want to show us the normality of interabled relationships. Inclusiveness is important to them. They want to teach this to their new baby. Their huge smiles show their happiness.

These inspirational people prove that people are not their diagnoses and that their worth is not based upon how others may view them. Many of us set limitations on ourselves. We can look at these people and realize that we can have rich lives and do wonderful things. We need to break boundaries set by ourselves and others and create our dreams!

Maybe after "meeting" these incredible people living great lives, we may be more caring and accepting. There is an easy way to help people with or without differences—be nice! Each day we have a choice. Do we want to be at the round table and starve or will we use our long spoons to help others and thrive? In a world that can be unkind, we can choose kindness and help—little by little, one by one.

We can open our hearts and minds to see all of a person. Get to know them, all parts of them. Break through a shell, theirs or yours. Be open and loving. We are all incredible.

My good friend has confidence in creating goodness. Instead of "Have a great day," she quotes Frosty Westering, "Make it a great day!" Much more powerful. Babies may not seem very powerful, but how many people say a sweet smile from a baby makes their day brighter? That's power. We can make a great day for ourselves and others. Would you like to feel good and important? Change a life for the better. Don't you feel great after getting spontaneous help or a sincere compliment? Listen to a sad or lonely person. Smile. Do a favor. Give a compliment. Invite someone to sit with you. Be brave. Go out and be yourself. We have choices. We have power. Make today great!

In loving memory of my dear friend
Darla Jean Lamb

A modified version of Darla's story is
available in a children's book.

DIFFERENT, YET LIKE ME: DARLA

Book One in a children's series designed to
provide a better understanding of how illnesses,
disabilities, and differences affect people

Information is available at lookbeyondpublications.com.

*If you have a difference and might like
to be part of this series of books,
please let me know at mary@lookbeyondpublications.com*

About the Author

Mary Salz grew up in the arid Southwest among cacti, mountains, and stunning red rocks. She now lives in the Midwest amid green trees, deer, and her two delightful children. She credits her mother and Darla for inspiring her active volunteer life. Hosting the school snakes for a summer was her most "Am I out of my mind?" yet fun experience. Like most authors, she loves to read. Her favorite activity is dancing, to almost any kind of music, one of God's greatest gifts!

Are you interested in contacting the author?
Would you like questions for a book club meeting or the children's version of Darla's story?

lookbeyondpublications.com or marysalz.com

www.ingramcontent.com/pod-product-compliance
Lightning Source LLC
Chambersburg PA
CBHW032054040426
42335CB00037B/713